# ESP32 PROJECTS FOR

# BEGINNERS

## Example Code, Arduino, Alexa Control, Thingspeak, Projects And More

By

Janani Sathish

# TABLE OF CONTENTS

# GETTING STARTED WITH ESP32

It started with understanding what exactly is ESP 32 and why we are going to use one to create applications. Well, the common convention will always see that use. The 32 is a microcontroller, but you should always remember that it's much more than just a microcontroller. In fact, it's a complete system on CHIP or S or C as we developers use to college. Now, why this insourcing? Why not the usual already nodes or extreme 32 of those kind of controllers? There is a reason for it. The system on CHIP needs an integrated package of a microcontroller, a very big amount of flash memory and coupled with Bluetooth and Wi-Fi. And I built on the same chip with an engine. Now, because of that, what happens is ESP 32 becomes a very ideal choice whenever you want to create any connected applications or connected system project for the exec, any kind of applications created, particularly for applications. If you want to have a look at the features of ESP 32, I'm not particularly giving it away here because it's much better to see it onto the official website itself. So I'm going to open the official website that is expressive. The developer of ESP 32 CHIP and on the same website will try to see what are the different features available into it. What microcontroller is there? Is it ARM or is it something else then? How many pins are there and what exactly it is better to do? The purpose of this session is to understand what is the ESP 32. We are not going to look into the modules, but just the USP 32 I see itself. So this is the page of ESP 32, the official website of expressive systems, and this is the language of ESP 32 CHIP. Now, what exactly is this better to do and how expensive creates them? You have to understand this thing first before we try to use it. So ESP 32, as we were saying, primarily is an associate order system on CHIP, but expressive also sales. The modules created at launch is better to do, which makes it easier to use them.

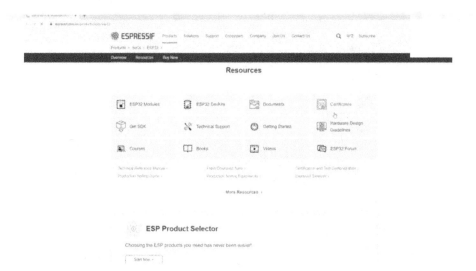

Overview    Resources    Buy Now

## Resources

ESP32 Modules          ESP32 DevKits          Documents          Certificates

Get SDK               Technical Support       Getting Started     Hardware Design Guidelines

Courses               Books                   Videos              ESP32 Forum

Technical Reference Manual >      Flash Download Tool >        Certification and Test Certification >
Production Testing Guide >        Production Testing Equipments >    Download Selector >

More Resources >

### ESP Product Selector

Choosing the ESP products you need has never been easier!

Start Now >

Now you can see you can either have ESP 32 modules or you can have your SU 32 decades documents. Everything is original here. Now, if I go to USP the 32 modules, then I will come to a different page and here you will see what are the different ESP 32 modules which are available. The most popular one which we use we are going to use in this project. Also, it's called This is better to do drum set or w r w m Sivits. Now there is a document for this from CID. It's I don't want you to download it. I don't want you to have it. We are just going to discuss it over here because we don't want to go into the exact technical details of the module itself. So I have this module in front of me. Let me finish. This is the module that I should use with 32 from 32 or 32. So what we are interested in is the primary features of this module, how it looks like.

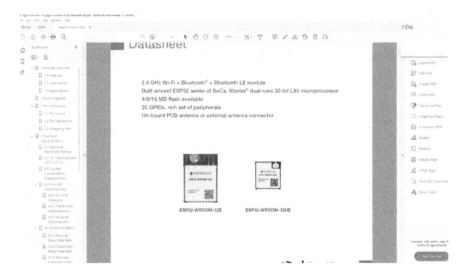

So the module looks like this. As you can see, this is not just the system on chip, but it's a complete module which consists of the antenna as well. So it is built around the ESP 32 series of SLC, which is having an extensive dual core 32 bit microprocessor that a number of different flash chip available or flash options available. Primarily the one we use is either A10 B flash or 16 MP flash, which is quite good. Then this module is also having 26 GPUs, all general purpose input output pins. Let's go into the details of this chip and its features so you can see that a number of different peripheral support for design for this module, you can interface SD card and SPI, there is UART, then there is a still eye to see BW motor problem. Then I in front edge but it's counter means timer counters use then the input pin Sophia's filter to do so having capacitive touch inputs we have we do see DSC as well as this additional protocol to WPI. Overall, it's a complete package where you can utilize or connect most of the current and latest embedded interfaces. If you look into the if you look into the Bluetooth side or wireless side of it, so it has got 2. 4gigahertz Wi-Fi and Bluetooth center frequencies, 241222484 megahertz DVI phase it 02. 11 big end, which is supposedly the latest one. Supports 150 Mbps of data transfer, and we have both Bluetooth version 4. 2 as well as Beat. And the applications are literally limitless with this particular chip. And most important reason why this is so popular around the world is definitely because of the cost. It's a combined package. You don't need a

6

microcontroller and a wireless device to be interfaced with each other and then start building your application here. You can create your application directly from this module. Now, as you can see closely, this is just a photograph for representation. But if you look at it closely, you can see it's a module. Okay. So it's an assembly of surface mounting type module? I don't think so. You can directly use a module that unless you are very good at solving and all the things. So what do we need? Whenever something like this is there, what we need something extra. Just a module will not do for us. So what I will need or what we believe is let's say this is split into two module, then it will need look many different things along with it. So you're going to required a USB interface to download the code. Then you are going to required power supply for this board. Then you are going to require some peripherals. With this fold. Now, what people or manufacturers across the world are doing is they are taking this institute model and then creating a model of their own. So the heart is the hospital to the room. I'll show it to you on hardware. Don't get confused. And then something like this, it's created around it. Like I said, this is called s e s p 32 node MCU. Now, similar to that, I'm just giving you an example of node MCU. But similar to that, there are a number of different modules built around E. S We 32. And if you open any, any electronic stores, for example, in India, let me open Rowboat in, which is one of the most popular stores. So if I open that and for that matter, any such online store and if you search for ESP 32, you will be overwhelmed with a lot of different options. And that happens with everyone with starting to experiment with this series of devices. So I just search for is the 32. And if you look at the results, there are lots of them.

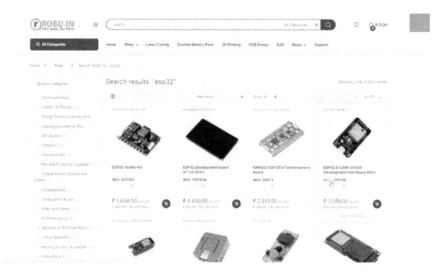

So nano use with 32 years for 32 audio is for 32 can 18 node MCU yes v 32 OLED module dpkg you see. And you know, what happens is all of this will get very soon. Very quickly, confusing to you? I'm not saying you cannot use any of them once you understand, once you learn how to use this better to do, you can choose any one of these modules and start creating your project. Even the direct models are also available, as you can see here. But to get to that stage, we need to set a common ground. And for the sake of training project, I have to choose the kind of module which is available here in India, as well as my friends who are taking this project in South Africa or China or in America, in European regions, everywhere. I need a kind of module which should be required or which should be available almost everywhere around the world. Only then we can set a common ground, because previously it has happened with me the same kind of node MCU, which is available over here, maybe available in a different package somewhere else, although they are cheaper. But the standardization is not there. And that's what makes it difficult to use a board for a project. We need something standard so that whatever we teach here should be easily replicable at your age. And to do that, what we do is we use this approach whose are 32 brought it. We just go to it and just Google it in the fruit. So 32 because I want to show you the official page on Aeroflot website. Now, also 32 is an EESP 32 board created by end of route. Now in the throat, I guess we all know about it.

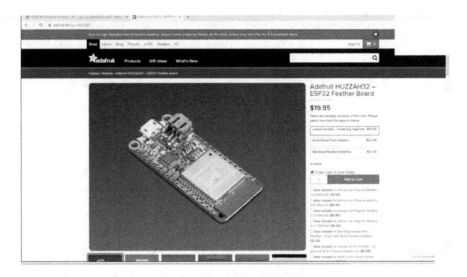

If you don't know about it means the early end of the simply getting started within. But Systems and effort is a New York based company which creates a lot of different hardware's a lot of different tutorials as well as the cell number of different devices tubes development board the other kids now is maturity is something which is created by end of the call it is better to do Thunderbird now we are going to use this throughout our project. What is the reason for it? The reason is very simple. The same board is available almost across the globe. Anywhere you go you can get to support and if you can't get this, what you can directly order it from it of it. I don't want to go into the complexities of some of your design. These boards, which may be available today, may not be available tomorrow and can still get stuck. No, we want something standard and that's the reason we are going to choose this particular module. The features are listed here itself. If I zoom in the page, which it has got a 240 megahertz dual core microcontrollers integrated for 120GB of RAM, which is huge for microcontrollers for me. Flash integrated Wi-Fi dual Bluetooth onboard anti now low noise amplifier is in so we'll see why it is used ten capacitive touch interfaces. This is a 32 kilohertz oscillator for RTC. There are three watts, three SBI to A to C 12. It is inputs to two is and to this. Of project, these are all on paper specifications. When you are using the wi fi on DSP 32 chip, you may not be able to we may not be able to use all the features binding we are going to use. E we told you to

9

choose our model by end approach. I have a board with me. Let me show that to you. If you can see this is the is better to do with the module that I have. So it's not going to get focused of support. That's what I am doing and remove that module and just shoot from you will lose up to two further. Okay. So this is the same one that we're going to use here, which you can see in the beach over here. Look at it. This is the back side. This is the backside of my boat. So there should not be any kind of confusion whenever we are experimenting on your splitter. However, if you are confident enough, then you can apply the same learning to any of the other custom boards. Also, it is my recommendation to use this board because my experiment will be done on this page. I hope things are clear for you. So wherever you are, just search for your speed. 32. Who is 32? In your country you will find this center near you and grab a couple of boards.

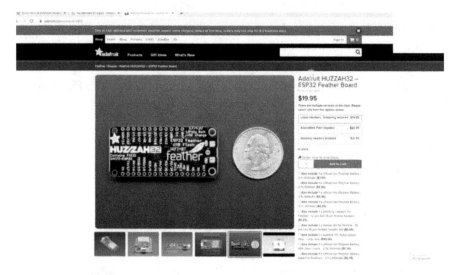

Why? I see a couple of boards because if you are just getting started, most probably you will make mistakes. And when you make mistakes, you immediately find the board or damage on the board. So it's always good to have one more extra at your hands. It never it is never harmful. And in my experience, you will immediately get started with your first board, probably do something, install in your home or sell it as a project. And you will want the another board for sure.

# GETTING TO KNOW ABOUT ESP32 BOARD

Let's get started with understanding a bit deeper about the aid approach with the 32 or 32 modules that we have selected and we are going to use throughout this project. As I've explained to you before, also the module makes it easier to use the actual USP 32 chip. So this gives you access to power supply, USB interface. The number of ports are very nicely laid out outside. You can see in my board these are the number of pins which are available over here and you will have easy access to them. That's why we use the module and we are going to use this in a module. As we have discussed this already, there are lots of different models available which may cause a lot of confusion. So we prefer to use ESP 32. So these are the pictures of the front and back side of this module. When the pins like this are not soldered. Okay, you need to sort of dispense by yourself so that you can inserted into a breadboard for experimenting. Now, let's see what exactly what are the things which are available on the ease with which it could support? Let's try to understand the hardware perspective. Very clear.

## ESP32 Huzzah

I want you to focus and understand the session very well, because it may happen that throughout your programming you may be trying to use some particular pin and switch. It is not behaving as it should according to a code. The reason being some of the pins are not useable when you are using file. So just get a clarity about this thing. The entire clarity about the board, although what we can observe here is this is the better connector used with introducer also comes with an onboard battery charger. You may find it a little bit expensive, but considering the utility, it's great. You can directly connect any lithium ion battery, which is 3. 7 volt treated directly to it. And it can start using or you can start using it as before to hit the connector USB cable to this beam and the battery will also get charged. So this is the biggest advantage of having the use with the support. Apart from that, we can notice the USB port interface here. Then there are two tiny bits which you can see over here. This is a reset push button. Then there are some ices over here and this is the exact one. If you turn over your board, then you can also see, because it's an eight effort board there, it's absolutely one of the biggest name in the creation of embedded hardware. Everything is very nicely laid out and written over here. Even the alternate functions. So this experience I do see the CLP as well as the number 22. This is a step in as well as the number 23. So a very detailed care has been taken by the float while creating the sports so as to make our life easier. Let's get started. Now these are the power points on the ECB 32 board. So whenever you have the board in your hand, you have to hold it with the antenna on the right hand side. If I turn it over, you will see it in live concert. But when I observe it like this, from my point of view, it is on the right hand side. So then I'm looking at it like here the pins. Exactly. Besides, the battery connector are back in.

# Pinout of Adafruit Huzzah32 → GPIO

And you ask me, these are some of the power pins which are used to power up the is the 32 and on the bottom you can see three volt and ground pin. Now, when you're using a usb-c connector, you don't need to worry about any of those things. There is a power supply on it which generates the 3. 3 balls and it is given at this point, if you are not using battery, then you don't need to worry about distance either. We'll discuss that later on when we try to use battery. So just ignore these three pins and instruments whenever you're trying to interface anything with your speed, touch and ignore them positively. Because if you connect something different over here, you may end up frying your chip and you will not even understand it. So just ignore the spins for sure. Next you can see the usable, simple general purpose eye opens on Twitter. What do you see on this slide? What do you see on the current slide? It's all the pins which are directly usable without worrying about anything being number 13, pin number12, 27, 33, 15, 32 and 14, and then a078283, even a five. So you can use these pins for sure without worrying. We'll discuss about those analog input pins later on. So these are the digital outputs and then these are the analog inputs. Apart from that, we have a secure ACL here and the exotics here will discuss about them. So 20 185848278380 1312 2733 1532 four. These are the pins. Now, why I was a little bit slow down in telling you about analog pins. The reason is here. Is it open is an analog input bin and also an analog output that is called

DC two. If you turn it over. That is mentioned there. Yeah, it is mentioned clearly the AC one, the AC two. And like that. Look at here. So this is the DSC to the AC one, things like that.

## Top Row

13 - This is GPIO #13 and also an analog input A12 on ADC #2. It's also connected to the red LED next to the USB port

12 - This is GPIO #12 and also an analog input A11 on ADC #2. This pin has a pull-down resistor built into it, we recommend using it as an output only, or making sure that the pull-down is not affected during boot.

27 - This is GPIO #27 and also an analog input A10 on ADC #2

33 - This is GPIO #33 and also an analog input A9 on ADC #1. It can also be used to connect a 32 KHz crystal.

15 - This is GPIO #15 and also an analog input A8 on ADC #2

32 - This is GPIO #32 and also an analog input A7 on ADC #1. It can also be used to connect a 32 KHz crystal.

14 - This is GPIO #14 and also an analog input A6 on ADC #2

**SCL, SDA** – I2C Pins

So is it is that. It can also be used as GPIO, and when you use it as a GPIO, you need to refer to it as spin number26 about PIN number even A1. Again, it is analog input and output, which is DSC one. If you want to use it as a general purpose input output pin, you can use it as pin number 25. Now PIN number A2 A3 if these are purely analog input, pin or general purpose input. So this is an analog input and also GPI. There is no output facility on PIN number eight to A3. And if that's the reason why I was telling you this is very important, please pay close attention. Then PIN number A5. This is an analog input pin and also GPIO four. So if I was analog input and GPIO for a two, three, four are analog and digital input only is true even are analog input and output, digital input and digital output prints. So this is all dispenser structure and then there are pins over here which are addicts and tags and pin number 21 is a general purpose input output pin. Now, the important thing about the analog twins, that's really, you know, one of the one of the very important thing is when you're using wi fi, when you're using a device, which we are anyway definitely going to use, then you can only read the analog inputs on it to pin because all other pins are shared with my family. Just understand that the Ethiopian can only be used as analogue inputs. Of project, not even digital output when you're using the. And my five facility that is provided by this chip. Now, apart from this fence, there is a circuit in my which is over here. You can see a circuit and a mine. This is these are the pins for a second speed. Protocol generally requires four miles. The fourth one, it sits on a chip select. You can use any other peanuts, Chip. Sell it for your spi peripheral. Then there is the exotics, which are the on chip. You want pins pin number 21 a general purpose digital input output. Then on the top side, you can see from PIN number 13. This is also an analog input it well there's also connected to the red LCD next to the device reports. These things are very important. When we are starting to use a microcontroller or when we are starting to use these people, we have to understand which includes two entity, which one goes to analog, which then goes to digital and with ADA Fruit also 32. All those things are very properly little. Then the pain we had besides it has been number 12. It can be used also as an analog input, calling it a 11. This bin has a pulled out adjustability which we recommend using it only at output only or making sure that the pull down is not affected during boot. So let's try to understand that PIN number 12 has to be used only for output purpose. PIN number 27 is also an analog input. PIN 18 on it is to do as the list should be. IO 33 is GPIO 33 also an analog input pin in nine? Now pin number 15 is GPIO 15 and analog input pin it 32 is GPIO 32. Also an analog input pin called a seven. Now this still pins can also be used to connect a 32 kilohertz crystal for on chip artist. In that case, if you are using it, then you will not be able to use this princess GPIO. And lastly, PIN number 14 is there which is also an analog input pin is six, then a cell is there are idle spins only and it is recommended that you do not try to use them as a digital input output. But all in all, you have to understand one thing, that when you are using the ABC a sort of ribbon, you are using device five facility, you can only use analog pin to. Now, this is a very nice representation of the entire board.

What each person does, what is the function of your screen? So you can see GPIO 21 and 17 and 16 are just primarily that it so 17 takes. 16 exotics, you can use them. Then the SBI pins is secure. It can also be used through programming as GPIO calling it GPIO 1918 N5. If I pin here what you see is a file and GPO for if you want to use it and this is also touch input. So this is very important and the standard water instrumentation, this will be the main central point of reference point for us when we do experimenting, when we when we create this kind of things in our laps or when we are working on this kind of things in our lab. What we usually do is we take a printout of this particular screen, take a printout of this particular thing because we need it. We are going to need it throughout our experimentation. Where do we connect? What we are to teach and where do these where to do that and all this sort of things? I guess this is pretty much clear to you and enough for you to grasp. This image will also be provided. Additionally, if not, there is a present in the presentation that I'm going to share with you.

# THINGS NEEDED FOR THIS PROJECT

Before we started using the EESP 32 to support me in approach here. It's something I would like to tell you. This is a very simple list of all the things that we are going to need throughout this project. You have to understand that on purpose. I have this list too small because I don't want you to spend a lot of money into just purchasing things and probably never use it. So I am giving you a list of very inexpensive stuffs. Apart from the an effortless to. You're also motives that probably all of the things which are shown in this list except in a proposal to the board, will come probably at the same price of list, price of data, proposal, board itself. So what are you going to need is a micro USB cable.

## Peripherals Needed for This Course

- Micro USB Cable x 1
- Adafruit Huzzah32 Feather Board x 1
- Bread board x 1
- Few LEDs
- Tactile button / switches
- Relay Module
- DHT22 Temperature and Humidity Sensor
- HC-SR04 Ultrasonic Distance Sensor
- A digital Multi meter
- Connecting Wires

Probably you have language around in your home, which is used to download programming details other to do with the report that you're going to need. Of project a break, but it's not mandatory but recommended in order to understand. Well then you need do it is for interfacing. Factory buttons are suggests to be used as input. You need a really model to experience the output part of it. Whenever we are going to turn a real life device, we are going to use. Really. I will show you what kind of really module are needed as required, but just want you to have a notebook. Then they are going to use two simple sensors to do temperature and humidity sensor and it's a subtle zero for ultrasonic distances. So these are very cheap and inexpensive and available almost everywhere around the world. And apart from that, having a digital divide, my mustimeter and some connecting labs is always an added plus. So that's all that you're going to need for this project.

# GETTING STARTED WITH ESP32 INSIDE ARDUINO

Hi. Let's get started with actually downloading some sample programs into this fruit south32 board. Now, in order to do that, what we need to do is we need to install the Arduino in the computer and we need to add this board in the board manager of Arduino. I'm considering you have not done anything before. If you have done something on already know much better, it will give a good heads up. But even if you have not done anything, no matter, we'll just do it. Everything right here from scratch. So just let me give you what we want to do. We want to install Arduino in our system, and then we have to add this link into the preferences of Arduino, which will be able to download the inspector to the board. So let's get started. I'll first go to Arduino dot CC and we'll try to download the Arduino software if you have it already. No need to do it again. I just got to software.

And I will download the latest Arduino IP. So Windows seven seven and newer best ways to download and install. If you want to donate something just to me, do it annually. So I'll just to download. And now the Arduino software package will get downloaded on your system. Was there already? No installer is downloaded on your computer. All you have to do is just double click the installer file and let your dino get installed. Also remember when they already it's being installed, make sure to click yes to all the driver installation that it will ask you for. Just start the installation. And I will say yes to any drivers it asks me to install. Just too. I agree. Next, keep the default location. XT and let it get completed. It shouldn't take more than 2 minutes depending upon your computer, but even on much simpler systems, much tinier systems also it doesn't take much time. Alternatively, you can also use alternate clouds, but we prefer having the programs offline on our computer. So even if you don't have access to Internet, which doesn't happen nowadays, but even if you don't have the Internet access, you would be able to use the programs that you have. It happens sometimes the nature connections get large that it's a problem, and Internet may take an hour for it to restore. And meanwhile, you want to work on something important. So best way is to have everything offline. But conventional thinking. But yes, it is. So already the installation is completed. It has not asked me to install any drivers because in my computer all the drivers are already there. But it will

19

definitely ask you if you are doing the installation for the first. Now let's open the original. And next step is if I go to this presentation, you can see. The next step is to add below link to the preferences of Arduino. We'll see what is preferences. But first, I'll copy this link completely. And now insert or, you know, go to file. But Francis. Here you can see additional border manager orders can be. Installed here. So whatever was there previously? I do not know if it is a blank installation. There would be nothing I have just reinstalled by uninstalling. Therefore I can see some previous stuff. So I have completed this link here and pasted it the same one from the presentation. So all you need to do is just do this file. Click. Okay. Now. What tools? And board manager.

And then you will be able to search for ESB to. Now, you see, it's better to do this already installed on my computers. As I told you, I removed the Dino and reinstalled it. Therefore, the board definitions and everything remains the same over here. Still, what I'll do is I'll try to install the latest one, which is 2. 0. 1. Remember installing XP 32, Bolt is installing a completely new French compiler altogether for use by32. So it may take some time. As you can see here it is 148. 976 KB It means one almost 149 maybe you can see, which is not a very small slice to download. Therefore just wait for it to be completed and then will continue with the experiment. Another download has been completed. It will take its own time depending upon your Internet speed as well as the speed of your computer. Download and then install the ISP through the works. Meanwhile, what you can do is if Arduino it's connected to your computer. So this is micro USB cable I'm having, which is required for the ISP 32 support to work. So I'll just connect the cable over here. And if I have a driver installed, then you will hear a beep. Which you can do is go to device manager on your computer. And see if you can see a complete coming up. Now see silicon labs sleep 210 Excuse me to divide bridge. This one is a complete funnel rDNA. Now what I'll do is or is better to do with Zavod. Not always remove my original. You can see that one world has vanished. So whenever you connect it, you'll get to see the complete number. If it is not coming up, it means you need to install drivers for this. You split 32 or 32, but most of the times the drivers are already installed. But if they are not, then you can simply search for speed. 210. To use what we what bridge drivers, it is very straightforward and simple to find and you can install it. Let's see. The Arduino board installation is completed. Now, what I'll do is I'll try to use or I'll try to select. The article is better to do bold or huzzah authority to board from the board manager and I will tryto download a blink program. Let's see. So in your original installation, by default, if you go to tools and if you go to bold, you willfor sure see Arduino as your default board selected for the fresh installation. But when I go to this option here, I can see I have already know if you are boards and then there is32 Arduino boards. Now what we want to do is we want to go to ESP 32 bolts audience for 32 original boards.

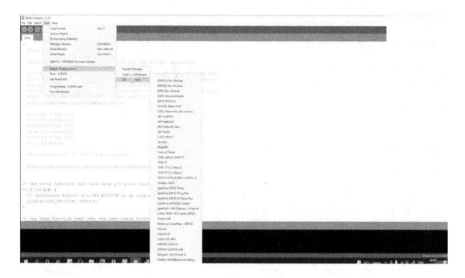

And we want to find out this particular board here. Our depth route is to do feather in the fruit is better to do feather. I have selected the ADA Proteus with 32 Federal Board on every Arduino board. You know that there is a built in LCD. Sometimes it is connected to pin number 13 on it or do not know in case of board like was that 32.

You can see it here, the onboard LCD. It's connected at Richmond. Let's try to find out over here. So I guess it's some had discussed it. So on this Saturday to further about the LRT, there is an on board you can see over here, which is a red colored one, a followed on. It's connected to pin number 13. So also it is it and touch input. Let's try to read the program footage. So this is a convention meeting or do you know that the building is referred as the building? Whatever is aboard it will try to get rich, but we'll just try to make it 13. If you are not aware of the typical Latino programming set up, then and every original program consists of two primary things. So what is called a void setup and another one is called void loop. What a setup. It's something that executes only once and void loop. It's something that includes forever. So whatever you write, don't end. World Loop is your main program that you need to be looped in continuously forever. Let's say it's the temperature logger on the cloud. So you want to read temperature? Send it over to cloud. Let's say wait for 5 seconds against the temperature. Send it over to cloud for 5 seconds. So this should come in your loop. But in order to use the temperature sensor, in order to connect to the network, you need to do some initialization that you will do in void setup. If you are completely unaware of the coding structure of Arduino, don't worry. As we go on, we will try to understand things easily. So first thing we need is our first thing we write is in setup we write bin more 13 comma output and then we wrote in our loop digital right 13 comma high digital right 13 comma low. Now that's a very simple blank program that I'm going to do and I will save it as let's say I'll just create a folder on my desktop, I'll call it is with 32 codes. I'll just call it Blink. I have saved this. What I'll do is just to make things simpler. Keep the delay of 2 seconds. Now we're all set. The Last 432 board selected. Then you need to select this comport again. Look at your silicone laps use, but divide bridge, come set content. So select content in the ports. And then you're ready to upload the code. Just click on this button upload and you will see the code will start uploading onto the board. There is a narrative which is fostered when the code has been downloaded. I'll show you that. But first, let's see how the court downloads and how we can see the output on our entity. So you can notice the state associate for now. What it is doing is it is trying to compile the sketch was the sketch compilation is done. It will try to upload that onto the Feather 32 or ESP 32 Effort Board. Let's wait for a couple more moments so you can see the progress. But here you can see the progress. Message is here, let it get finished completely and then we'll be able to see. Now see it is uploading, connecting the writing, writing, writing, writing a lot of statistics, leaving hardly sitting. Where is it now? You can see the court is downloaded. Can you notice the only blinking with a delay of 2 seconds? On for 2 seconds. For 2 seconds and for 2 seconds. Offer 2 seconds. Look at it. You. Now, this is the lady that I was talking about, which appears or which blinks when you're trying to download a code. Now, what I'll try to do is I will try to reduce the delay to 500 milliseconds, and I'll try to upload it once again. Now you'll see. Well, applauding again, this lady will be blinking continuously or very fast. Now it is compiling the sketch for now. This is the foster. Mostly this is uploading. The uploading process had started. It's finished. And now you can see the blinking faster. So this is the first and most important thing that you will do whenever you get a new Arduino board. So I hope this is clear to you how to do this processes. The presentation is given to you in which you can copy the link from.

# SERIAL COMMUNICATION BASICS ON ESP32

Hi. In this edition, we'll try to understand how to perform the communication between ESP 32 and a computer. Now, definitely there would be a question why we want to work with Syrian communication first. And I do experiment a lot with all the projects that I create. And I have found that working with Syrian communication first clarifies a lot of

## Why?

- Easiest output device
- Can print text of any length
- Gives a quick way to print data
- Simple to use

different things and it gives you an easy and quick output device to start working.

Besides, the libraries and vaults are simple to use, and therefore I think starting with Syrian communication would be a good point for you into the world of yes, we have to do embedded systems and , so let's get started. First of all, let me get back to the basics of serial communication. So in order to understand that, what I'll do is I'll try to open my white book because it gives me quite a good. Well, space to explain things. Okay. So let's get started. When was this initial communication? What we want or what we mean needs? It's whatever microcontroller you have. In this case, we have 32. But it doesn't matter which one it is. So whatever microcontroller you have has to communicate with computers. And why do we need to do that? Because serial communication is the simplest way to communicate between devices of Syrian interfaces like computers, but not limited to only computer. In the same way, you will be interfacing to a Bluetooth module. Sometimes you also interface with other interface ships and like many different peripherals like ships, GSM. RFID reader and so on. Now with respect to computer, there is one issue computer doesn't have. I mean, at least the laptops doesn't have of making cereal. So what we do is we use a USB to cereal interface. And the beauty with every Arduino compatible board, including the ES with 32, is it comes with anon board USB interface. So an alias with 30 to work if you're looking to do schematic, I have some very indisposed version here

because if you look at here this I see over here speed 102 or 2104 is useful to you on bridge.

So the microcontroller will communicate with this ESI using two lines or less. SD And you can see those two landscapes as well as you. We send the data using the DMZ line, using asynchronous communication, and we assume they talk to the Annex two line on the controller. This I see acts as a bridge to interface with the USB port of your laptop or your computer. Would you ever use it? So things become simpler in this city when you try to interface with this. However, there is one thing to understand, and that is this is all synchronous communication. Primarily this it's asynchronous means launch. In asynchronous communication that is not block share between EESP 32 and the computers. On any communicating device. So the clock is not shared. And because of that, we don't have a way to synchronize between the bits which are being sent. What I meant

26

to say is if I'm sending something like this, then. Is this single one on? This is 1101 or this is 111001. We don't have any means to identify that. What is exactly one? What is the duration of one? What is the duration of zero? We don't know that we cannot synchronize because the clock is not synchronized. And because of that, what we do in asynchronous it in communication, it's synchronized with this speech. A very simple example. It's I'm pretty sure you come across people from lot of different geographical backgrounds, a lot of different places. And you may have observed that some of them have a tendency to speak faster, probably, or speak slower. Now, when you work together, when you become friends for the first time, would you say to each other is you talk to him or her? That means go a bit slower. He or she talks to you that is going faster and adjust your communication speeds in the exact same manner. What we do is we match the speed at both devices. This speed is called let's mix for a second. Which. Also called outrage. Now, there's a lot second thought about it. There are some standard definitions by IPC which are used. But the most popular one, it's mentioned zero zero which is being used and top of the land. It is 115200. So you can see that the communication is happening at one of the explosive objects most commonly. However, it is not limited to you can use any if you want. So what we have to do is we have to set the scene which split second voltage at the transmitting or one device and the same one at the other device so that internal clocks are synchronized with each other and therefore whatever data is in sent, it will be properly identified. So it may very well be the case that this is 111110000. This is one one. Doesn't matter. Whatever is the detail sending, it will probably be synched between the two devices if the mode matched. So this is what we're going to do and we can perform two way communication in it. There are a lot of different things like Blix will replace, but I will not go into those intricacies because those are not important to you. What we can do, however, here, is understand one thing that we have two separate lines density and objects so we can transmit and see, but not at the same time. Usually it is half the communication. And you can also do it at the same time, also in some cases. So let's start get started with understanding of a simple program on serial communication with DSP 32.

# SERIAL DATA PRINT USING ESP32

Now that we have got some understanding of the serial communication, let's see what are the different library functions available in order to perform the system communication? So what I've done is I have listed some of the most widely used or you can see most used function here. However, the library's quite comprehensive. I'll also show you that where

## Serial Communication Library in Arduino

- begin ()
- write ()
- print ()
- println ()
- available()
- read()

you can see for the references and how to get a better understanding of all of the functions. But to start with, these are some of the functions that we are going to require that we're going toned.

So Serial or begin is a function which we will be using to start the communication. We need to specify objects on which you. Then civil rights is a function which is used to send a single byte on a serial device from microcontroller from USP 32 to the other device. Cylinder print function is a very nice function that you can bypass either a single byte, autocomplete, extreme, or even a variable. It will convert whatever you post which to ASCII and it will be sent to the other device. Similarly dated serial print Ellen which also prints a new line along with this asking that your percentage. Cylinder available is used to check if there is some data coming on the serial code for reception and still not read is used to read the data. Now without spending much time over here. Let's try to understand the program in action. So I just discard this and I'll open a blank. Or you know what, skip and start writing a program. Now lets start typing some code. As I said, the very first thing we need to do is Syrian docs begin. So Serial is the class name that we use and begin is the function. And here you need to specify about, for example, specifying 9600. It's a very common practice to give a small deal to get the serial module initialized. Well, so we put in, you know, ten milliseconds, 100 milliseconds. And in one of the what I like to do is I try to bring something on the serial. So serial French alarm, which will also present a new line. Welcome to ECP 22. The serial communication. And let's put a delay of, let's say, 2 seconds. So delay function here will give you the delay of a specified number of milliseconds. Let's try to save this score and see which in the same location so that you can have the access afterwards. And I will call it serial. Yes. Okay. Now, let's try to upload the score into the controller. So what tools? Select Board. We have selected it right then Select Board. We have selected it based upon our configuration and then upload the program compiles first. It is for data due to which compiler which is we have already installed on the audience. It usually takes some time to install, make sure that the board it's connected to a computer. I'm using a desktop system here. I do prefer it because things remain the same in the same place. So whichever you use it, just make sure the board is connected and now you can see the program is downloaded. Now we want to see this output. Where is it and where is it printing this? Welcome to yes. We try to do serial communication and all. So in order to see that we need a different software called this terminal, a terminal can open your serial ports, whether they are physical serial port like those are in desktop or later. Those are the US which are serial virtual homework which are provided by the boards like he is talking now. In order to do that, we have to use a different software but already provides a built in utility. It's called a serial monitor. If you can see it in tools, you can see serial monitor. You will find the same thing here. Also on the top right corner, look, two on the top, right corner. So if I click on this button, it will open the serial monitored. If you can see the serial monitor has opened and the data it's coming from microcontroller this you can see here the state is already selected as sensitive. But if I do choose something else, see what happens. So the data still coming, as you can see, but the computer is not able to interpret it properly. So some garbage values are shown. If I choose a lower power, if I choose a higher about which. Something. Same is going to happen if we don't understand what we're actually getting and losing. That's gombrich because the interpretation is getting it all. So in order to correctly interpret it unique, you use the same model which has been used in your program. When I see 9600, then you will see the text that is coming. Starts making sense. So this is the simplest way to send data to computers. Let's try to see something more. Let's say we have a variable. I declare a global variable for this purpose and I is equal to the zero. And let's say we want to print this variable on the input as well. So now what I do is welcome to serial communication. I equal. Instead of print. Ellen What I know is a blueprint only because it will then not print a new line. And I can print either just besides this line and then print it. You'll get it. And then sell the print and I. And then I'll simply do what? Hopelessness. So whenever the I it sense to see the import, it will be incremented by one. So I'll do control you, which is a shortcut for uploading the code on to the board. And you can see the compiling had started. If we could combine completely and then it will be downloaded onto the board. Uploaded to sea. Technically an already notorious Nazi. It's connecting the 1919, 19, writing, ranting. And so let's open serial port. Lucy Read started with one because the zero was already printed. In that case, what I do here is I just reset my board once. You see. Welcome to serial communication is equal to zero. Then one, then two, then three. Four. And so on and on. So this is how you can print of Feinerman onto the Syrian communication channel. I'll send a variable to Syria communication channel. One thing is interesting. The zero is actually a decimal zero. It's not ASCII. The Cyrillic print alone will convert it to s. However, if I don't see it elegant right then it will indirectness in zero as it is to the computer. And if I open a browser and if I look to ask it. Shocked. Then you will see in this ASCII chart Z2 is let's see what did zero so zero which startled me. Well. We see some of image. So zero is actually null. One is associated with something. Three, It's something and a lot of characters. After 48, it starts with one and they will get to zero and then onwards. So let's try it first. Let's see what happens when I write the zero one and so on, and then we'll try to see the other things. Cause I don't want to confuse you, but I do want to understand the difference between right and print and tell it. There's a reason why I'm giving you this example. One problem is there because it looks like it will not go into new line. What will do it? Settle down and just put in a blank new line for things to get easier because then it will come in the new line. So now it's compiling. Once it's uploaded, I just click to see monitors. Now you can see. So we are not actually sure. Okay. I just opened the board first, so I monitor first. So the photos are downloaded. That is Ed. Let's properly download the code and then only open this little monitor. This volume doesn't happen with the regular art in the works, but he we tend to do something different and it has been made to work with art. So certainly do art. Now the downloading is going on. Then open the cereal box. Nothing. There is a box again. A box again. A box solicited. Zero one, two, three. For. Five. Six with a delay of 2 seconds is coming. The first printable characters will be absurd at 33, which is you can see. Which is the exclamation mark before that. All of the characters are not going it. We cannot wait that long. So let me just start with something. Three settle and let's leave a delay of 1/2 and sort of. To. Let's see what happens after this code is downloaded. Now the uploading had started a lot on the Syrian port and soon as the downloading is uploading us to. Again, you'll see a box, but now you'll see the characters started coming in. So 1331 or maybe even 30, and then 31 and then 33 onwards. You can see the printable characters are coming. If we wait for a bit long, then we'll also start to see 48, 49, 50, 51, 52, 53, four, 55, 56and so on. So these are the decimals which, when directly given to a device for printing, will be interpreted as the obstacle and the respect to us. The character which is represented by that form will be printed. You will require this a lot in coming times. So just make sure that when you are printing a variable and you know, representing that you'll seethe bridge unless there is an explicit needed to your serial or light, don't use that. And when that comes, I'll tell you in the next project when we're trying to read something that looks.

# SERIAL DATA READ USING ESP32

Now that we have done with serial test, what I'll try to do now is I will try to create a serial lead program. Now let's started with some basics. Let's begin. 9600. We'll just have to meet with Larson because we took time to open the input. So it's better if we have a meatless or Delia. Then what we'll do is we'll try to do this. Now, I want to read it from cereals. So before I directly need a film cereal. But let me tell you how it works. So whenever you send something to the microcontroller, it is stored in a cereal buffer. It's kind of a temporary storage which holds whatever data is coming to the cereal box. Usually the forsythia's depends on the board you have but a very common factor on a very common name number on the cereal buffer of our DINO. It's 64 bytes or 156. So those are some of the common numbers you can go into the libraries to understand about them. But to get started, we don't need to worry about it. When time comes, I'll tell you about it. So the thing is data to us to send into this buffer and then only you can use cereal dot need in order to see this data. And if you don't have anything to read, then you will probably end up reading blank because there is nothing in the buffer. So therefore, in order to understand if the data is received or not, we need to have a function. The function in Syria is not available. So still not available is the function and it returns the number of bytes from the city. Okay. So if that is the case, then how do you use it? Using is very simple, actually. So if so, a lot of the label is greater than zero. What it means, even if a single character is really then this if condition is strong and will be executed. So if serial dot available is greater than zero. And then what we want to do is we need some variable to store this. So let's say entity is it will do city or not. Okay, so we read it in serial note. We're using serial or data function in table called a and then. Then what? We'll try to bring it back to the computer. Now, you have to understand that when you enter something from the computer, you have always entered ASCII. Even if you have entered zero, it means you're sending 48 and so on. And therefore, if I have to print it back to the computer, I should not use the interpreting function and instead I should see the look like function before I send it to B, C or Lewis I can delete and then I'll know what. Serial dot print e. The same man. And then when I lose it are not Ellen and the blank line. I'm sorry. I misprint here. It looks very much, as I mentioned. So whenever something is received after 3 seconds, the same might be sent back to the beast. Let's see how it works. Let's upload this code for now. And once the uploading is done, we'll try to see how it works. If you want, you can also do some hello welcome or something here which will indicate that the programmed started. The biggest advantage of serial communication, apart from the usage for system communication actually is debugging.

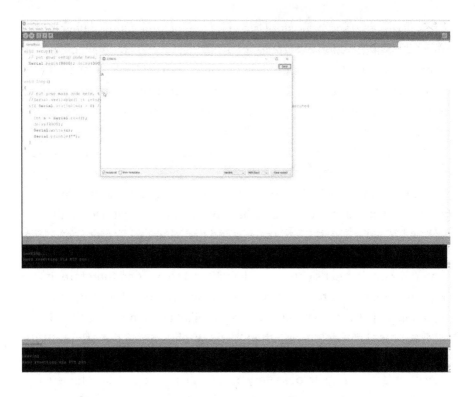

It's easy when you go into when you go in to creating advanced, advanced embedded systems. Many times you'll find a move that you don't know. A particular piece of code is being executed or you don't know if you have written some commands to learn something from something and you don't know whether it has been received or not. So in those places, you use the serial brain function as a debugging tool. We just think, let's say hello. Okay, I come up to here. I came up to there in your code in multiple places. This will help you a lot. And you'll find that experimentation. So the code is downloaded from the serial monitor and it started to bring something. So let me first view Capital E over here. So I have the capital E and I'll just click on the send button. 1 to 3 seconds. We've got the capital E back. Let me put zero here and cents. One, two, three. And we got zero over here.

So this is how you do it from Seattle port and you take it back. If you want to be a bit more experimental with what we do, then you simply do serial or write. It looks like this. Or what'll happen is if you have given zero, one, seven and eight in this country, you have given small C, then you will assume small B and so on. So these are the most common functions, most common ones which are useful serial communication. And. To get started. This is enough. Now let me give. Let's see. Capital B. And then after 3 seconds, one, two, three, after 3 seconds, we supposed to get an E, whatever you pass if I give one. And then after 2 seconds, I'm supposed to get something else. When you give the send button, then what happens is you also send a new line character from computer and therefore addition one to that is also disabled, which is why you're seeing this box. I'll you five here I have removed this sort of still option. Let's see. We got six and we got six. Only if you notice. Now what is happening is we are not sending an additional new line from computer with this auto store and therefore there's just a the single light. So this is the bare minimum that we are going to need with safety communication as we go forward. But there's something of the stool. It's basically just getting started. So if you just look Cardinal Health and reference over here. A webpage will be open to you, which shows all the Arduino functions, everything over here. Now, what we want to do is we don't want to go into all of these things. What we want to do is we want to understand in detail about what is clear celebrity and what are the parts of it. So serial.

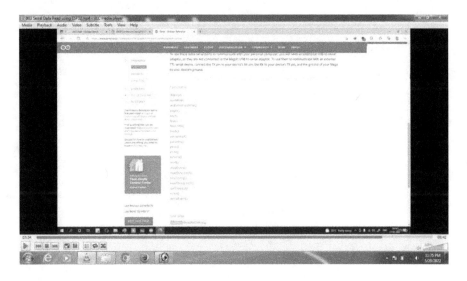

Now you can see the function list here. So if Syrians are available, available prior to beginning to find them, they'll flush us load funds. They

35

speak French. But in the land until a lot of different functions are due. We will use this functions as the time comes. For example, if you have to use the spots and function and you just click on that and you read the documentation, looks for the next while indentation and then come and see the function every time such as a serial or pass into inherits from some class and you'll see all the documentation we've written over here. As and when time comes, we'll see all those different functions with serial communication. You can also do device control over here by checking what is the value of this e and maybe turn on something, turn off something and things like that. So I guess that's a good starting point for you. It's in communication. We'll get started and will come back to, say, communication.

# DIGITAL OUTPUTS WITH ESP32

Hi. Now that we have seen how to simply do blinking of an LCD on the speaker to do, or whose authority would vary that route, let's try to understand what exactly happened over this approach. Now, to do so, I need at least a schematic model of something obvious to show. But before that, let me explain you what happens. So when we write in motor type output, as I explained to you before, this will make wind turbine walk as output. Now there are multiple different bins which are

mentioned on the board or even in this GPIO shape. So which one you should use? Should you use this ABC number or should we use the CPI number? So ideally and technically for most purposes, we will be using this guy or numbers with which the pins are very easily accessible in Arduino board. So first of all, 13 is what the CPI number that we are referring to in our program. Now, when you write pin more output, it simply means that PIN number 13 will act as output. It can drive, it can generate voltages. And the next question is what voltages? So when you write digital like PIN number 13, Carmi had never done that and it is true and high. But why? Because when you write the number in my height, then in 13 becomes 3. 3. That is the logic one. Voltage four. But those are the two on cross. All the use of the total chips. Logic one strands 13. 3 volts. And can you write that pin as low? It means the pin becomes zero. It means close to computation.

Now, when it becomes 3. 3, which the LCD turns on. Now, what does that exactly mean? Now, to understand that, let's try to see the schematic of BSP 32. Okay, so here I have the schematic of use with 32. Just try to look at this section over here so we can see there is a resistor and an LCD which are connected to IO 13. IO 13 is the PIN number 13, which we referred to. So when we write Digital Note My Heart, what happens is this thing becomes 3. 3 world. That is it as a stop. And the control of the reality is going to. This is the reality that we have observed. On to the. Bold. I can also show it to you now. It's working. So this has been number 13 here, which is blinking. It's this one here. Now, what it means is it means if it ever can connect like this on board, then we can also definitely connect multiple such entities apart from the outside of the books, and we can link them. So let's see what I'm talking about. For all this purposes, this what I'm going to do is I'm going to use an online socket to show you this schematics. I will also be including the schematics into the master presentation so that you don't have to worry about a lot of different documentation. So I'll play a few and a schematic there. Everything will be the single presentation final. For now, let's go to the schematic that I have tried to prepare. So this is how you can create a schematic. Now, this is only for connecting for relatives to ISP temperature, but likewise you can connect andthen it is on whatever it is you want. Give us an entity must be connected with this. It is registered to the pin of we touch it whenever you go high on that. When we become 3. 3, this one kit is still very limited. The current flowing to the entity to 2.

3 million peers and you're done all liquids you can connect this one, this one, this one. The control of the ammunition go to ground and all should come to the controller beam.

The placement of resistor is your choice. You can keep the first resistor of later of resistor first and later. Many of the designers, mostly newcomers, have a confusion that we have to have energy first, and then there is also we have to have the register first and then the end. There is nothing like that. I have just created this to make it simpler. However, just to make the point clear here, there is no difference in connecting it like this and it's the current only flows when you also disclosed. So it doesn't matter whether you connect that it is to before or later. What matters is you must connect the and it's still possible. Now, if you create a socket like this on a blade, but using LSD and resistor, then you will be able to blink for different entities at a time. Also, what kind of footage? See here. Here we have PIN number 12, 27, 33 and 50. I have checked all this can be used as a digital footprint and therefore you can use VIN number 12, 27, 33 and 15 now and you can modify your code accordingly. So let's try to create another program here. I will just try to close this one. Now, instead of referring to them as in numbers, what I'm going to do is I'm going to give them someflexibility, one and two. So that to do that with a simple just note integrity one is equal to. Well. And similarly copy paste it three more times. I use a mechanical keyboard, so I guess that will be a problem for you. You might be getting some ticks, but it will stay the nights when you write the code. 2733. 50. 27. 13. I'm using the 33 and 15.

I think that would be. Now if you are using 40 entities at a time or for that matter elderly is at the time, it doesn't matter. All you need to do is you need to do more of each. So more energy output.

Now in the similar context we will go on alluded to in addition and you have to make sure to make all of them work as outputting. Without that, you can not generate output on the spins. Now let's assume that I want to make all of those spins higher, enter time and then low after some delay. So what I do is I like digital, right? And even my higher again, I will do a lot of copy wasting and I expect you to do the same. Don't become a typewriter. Be able to grammars. Okay. A very classic cliche line used by software industry, but it is true indeed. So all of them made higher. And now all of them I'll make. No, I don't even like low multiple times and such. And now all I'm going to do is I'm going to download that into your speech review board. All I have to do is all the settings of there already enthusiast, etc. to further contain everything is there to just click on the upload button. Before that, you have to save to score. So they have created a folder for it. Let me call it for ids. So it's been saved. Now you will notice the yellow will blink very fast after the compilation is done. And then the quarter we were down. Now, as you can see, the program has been uploaded onto the board. And the one which was blinking before the bulletin had stopped. Now did spins. 1227 3315 are now blinking.

But no one quibble with it. I will have to create a schematic like this on it. So you need that distance and you did. And it is in order to create this kind of schematic when creating the project. I want things to be simpler for myself and faster so that I can demonstrate to you. That's what I'm going to show you, that I have created a very simple book. Okay, it looks like this. I have created this particularly for one purpose. I will share with you the schematic as well as the layout also so that you can create one for yourself. The benefit of this building is it has got. Let me take the camera out and I will explain it to you better. So as you can see here. It has. What? If it's over here, then I have got four switches. Then I have a really a buzzer that is LCD. That is a real time clock. There is motor driver. There are lots of interesting stuffs over here. So if I use this one, then it will probably make my life. Is it what I'm going to do? I'm going to insert this USP 32 into a breadboard so that I can take wires out of it. And I will make the connections. However, please note that the connections remain exactly like this. As you can see, I'm screwed. Just give me a moment and

I'll make the connections. Hi, Nancy. Kinsey. See, I made the connections from this into this and more towards my. An absolute vendetta to do. All I have done is common. The grounding of our way to the ground of divorce. Divorce, common. And then this four points over here in number 12, 27, 33 and 15 are connected to four different entities. My board might be getting a bit older, so the brightness of it is different. But you can see the difference. You can see the blinking I've used. Now let me try something different. Let me make it 505 hundred as my. Well, let's see if you can notice the change in attitude. The code is being uploaded. Now the campaigning is going on. And it's uploading, though. And the uploading. It's done. Did you notice over here in this window? Sorry. All of them are blinking halo, halo, halo with a delay of 5/2. So 500 milliseconds. So this is just for the understanding of how do we generate output on multiple spins on DSP to do to book and the upcoming sessions. We'll see how we can interface with buzzer relays, switches and like many different things.

# ACCEPTING LOGIC INPUTS, PULL-UP AND PULL-DOWN CONCEPTS

Hi. In this project, we'll try to understand how we can accept digital inputs from the hospital to do this. The inputs when I see it usually comes with a picture of a button, but will also try to understand what are the different digital inputs and what and how we can accept them on.

Accepting digital Input on ESP32

Yes, we tend to primarily the level of the solution, but yes, of project I'll first especially be centered around how to connect a button externally to BSP so that we can have a switch input. And then we'll try to understand how we connect to other digital inputs like coming from sensor or something like that. So let's get started now for the session. I will not be having any presentation, but I would like to open my white board for this because it will give me much more clarity. Explain. And I guess you would also find it easier to understand. So when you try to connect a switch to, let's say, any microcontroller, currently our discussion of scope is limited to ESD 32. But in general, this discussion is highly to almost all the microcontrollers that you have. Let's see, this is some particular field of microcontroller which you want to connect a digital input. Let's not use in number 13. Let's look at futures. Now, when we see we have to connect a switch, generally a socket like this will come in out of range. Okay. So there is a switch connected to the pin. Either the switch will go to some place, it can be either high or it can be either because a microcontroller can only understand the logic higher logic. We also discussed that the higher usually means the you see on the web of controller and low usually means the ground of the controller. So owing to the same discussion, if I connected to 3. 3 word. The precise. It's when I press the switch, then the pin should get 3. 3. Which. The problem becomes when you do not with the switch, what the microcontroller is supposed to know about this input. And this is really important to understand. You cannot keep the pin of your microcontroller floating, because if the pin is floating, it can be read as anything. It can be read as logic one, it can be read as logic zero. Or maybe you press it and it will forever remain. Logic one Unexpected things can happen in this situation, so you cannot afford to do that. You have to make sure that if the pin is not getting 3. 3, then it must be getting zero volt from somewhere. And how do we ensure that? It is very simple. The concept, it's called it's a free download. Put it down to the substance. What you'll collect the high value register from this point, then get towards account. Now what happens because of this tension as to what happens is very actually simple. The pin becomes connected to ground to this register. Therefore, the potential on the spin all the time. It's logic zero 11. When you press the switch for that moment, only 3. 31 gets connected to the spin. So it becomes logic one and a small, tiny party. Three or three ball two divided by ten Current lost switch, which would see I think would be very small not to worry about. So a small current will flow to this register towards crunch and the controller thing will the same logic one. The moment you lift this switch again, what happens to the point where it is disconnected and the controllers again poured down by the sister towards Crouch and it becomes Z. This is where you ensure that the pin will get closer to zero when the switch is not list. This concept is called its pull down resistor. Similarly if you are using or connecting your switch against ground. Then. You're supposed to use pull up register, which is. Like this. And the value should be the same. I'm bigger than. So when you press the switch, the pin gets zero potential. But when you do not place the switch, the pinions fold up. This concept is called Let's pull up the stress. The pain will remain high all the time because of this system being connected to 2. 3 world. The moment you press the switch, it will become the moment you release the switch, it will again become logic. 3. 3 which.

So understanding of this concept of pull up and pull down is important. Now what microcontrollers like already know what that is to touch you too. There are some internal pull up and pulled under tools also. So we may not need to connect them externally, but in a good industrial design, it's okay when you are using it for experimental purposes. You can use the internal pull ups and we'll see it help. But if you are planning to create a good industrial grade product, then you have to connect the external pull over, pull down does a step to ensure a smooth and seamless operation.

# READ DIGITAL INPUTS ON ESP32

Hey. Now that we have understood how we can use the switch and pull up our freedom configuration, let's try to connect the switch externally to ESP 32 and let's try to see how to use it. So in order to do that, what I'm doing is I am going to connect the two switches like this is with the two to work. If you are using a breadboard, then you can connect the two switches or keys like this as a slim, because I'm using a very simple interface boat which has got some switches on to it. So any delays in them? Nevertheless, this is how the connection should be. One switch, it's connected to PIN number GBI as well. And another one is Digital Yellow 27. Now, the other point of the switch is directly going to them. If we just make some corrections, this. We'll look at. So now this is how my switch connections are connected.

Now, you might be wondering why you have not connected any pull ups, because the yes, we are due to boot the white suit with internal pullups, which can be an effort now to enable them to see enough of them. So there is nothing much to explain. The rhetorically jump to the corner. So I have a new sketch artist program taken here. Seemed as a switch test. I have written it. Which test? Nurse stick word setup. And why. Look. And

I'll declare the truce, which is like this, in which one is equal to 12 and switch to is equal to 27. As you can see over here. So 12 and 27. Now in setup. What I'll do is I'll just initialize the serial box so that we can send some information on the sit footprint of this, which is first and then the next instructions, important sequence, pin mode, switch one comma input and pin mode, switch to command input. Now to understand one thing very accurately that when you specify input, it means the pins will by default be translated. It means you will have to connect an external pool of water. Don't if you have to use the input like this. Otherwise if you want. Connecting the switch like I'm doing. Then what we can do is instead of writing input, we'll just write down input, underscore, pull up. Now when you write input, underscore, what happens is the internal follow-ups to the switches are enameled and now in action. And because of this internal collapse, what happens? The different stage which is read all the time, it's high and only when the switch is pressed, then the status of the switch may become low. You release the switch, it again becomes higher. Now let's see how to detect that. And of project, the function is very simple. It's called digital root. Now I will use that in an if conditions. If digital did switch one, it's low. Then I want to do something. What? Let's see. Let's do similar print and then switch on. It's pressed. Let's take some B project. Now what it does is, what did we do? It's. It's very simple. Whenever you press the switch, this if condition will execute. And because it executes those said you will see some message on positive that could switch one expressed. Now we do the same thing for switch to no much changes in the program as such. So f digital will switch to is equal to equal to blue. Then let's French switch to its best. That's simplistic. Let's turn to see the output of this school, then upload the program. Now let me clear my desk. I also happen to have a light here, but I have cleared the desk a bit so that I can now show you the camera. Okay, there is an error. I missed semicolon here, so just please bear with my desk. It is usually always messy because a lot of gates and the connecting wires and everything out here. But I guess that should be okay. And you might be able to correlate with me when it comes to your work desk, when you are experimenting on electronic gadgets. The code has been updating, has been Stockton and it's done.

So I just opened the serial monitor and what I'll do is I'll just use the camera to show you the actual set that I'm having. Just a moment. So this is the setup I'm having. You can see these are the two switches that I have. I have connected the first one. And the second one to is Vince. Vince, the number 12 and the number 27, which you may not be able to spot that usually in this way. And that's why I have given you a schematic. Now I'm going to press the switch the switch one. Okay. And look at the switch one press as well as on to the sit in moment. So switch when pressed. You can see, as long as I keep it pressed with a delay of 600 milliseconds, the message keeps coming. So which one is blessed? I didn't judge press the switch to. You can see switch to express the messages coming and as long as you keep it pressed, the message will keep coming. You limit the messages gone. Again, let me try and switch one. Now, see, as long as the switch is pressed, the program keeps repeating itself. Now what we can do in order to make this not happen. Okay. What I'll do just now for some time is I'll just put it over here, the camera. Let's say I don't want this to happen. So then I press the switch one. It's continuously coming in and out of it, but it's still continuously coming in. I don't want that to happen. Now, in that case, what you will do. You have to understand that this delay is particularly given for the same reason. The primary reason for giving this delay is it induces a time which is required for a user to press and release the switch or for a single switch press.

Now, let us assume that if you have not had time, delay this to moment. Okay. No. I have downloaded the score. Remove the delay. Now, see, when I press the switch, what happens? Even if I press and immediately the message it has been executed. One, two, three, four, five, six, seven, eight times same. We switch two and it is unpredictable. The longer you keep it pressed, the more the data keeps coming. Why? Because the delay of press and release is not induced. So first thing, in order to ensure that it doesn't execute multiple times the added unit. And furthermore, if you don't want a rapid execution to happen at all correctly, what's happening? It is going into the slope of this condition. This particular code, it's executed, then a delay, and then it comes here. It again ticks back to the first condition. If it's straight true, then this is executed. Now I can do something to avoid it being deliberately executed altogether. What I can do is very simple. So just look at it. So while. Digital read. So which one is equal to or equal to low? I will repeat. Vitamins are basically I can put the empty semicolon like this opening and closing it once. I'm just writing a while loop, but I have not written anything in there. The same can also be replicated ads by simply give me a semicolon over here. I'll repeat the same thing. In this case there was switch to is low. I will just wait to see what happens as an output of this scopes. So let me focus back again on this sutures and how the setup, the completion had started. And the program downloading is also starting to stutter. So. The upload procedure is done. I will open the cinema monitor. Okay. Now I want to press the switch and I'm going to hold it. Okay. So this is the switch I'm going to press and I've pressed it. Now see, I have hold the position, but still the court is executed only once. It's not executing again. Same way. If I press it again, then it will be executed once and it is not waiting at the one condition as long as it is law. We don't want to do anything. We just wait here and then it's again, switch to release. Now you see, while releasing sometimes it may come back again because there is a D bounce in the switch press itself. But I hope you got the idea of how these things are managed. If you don't want the even the slightest delay that is happening, then you can add a bounce. Demands delay is a very small, you know, the time required for the contact to be completely made or to be completely open. So basically a switch is nothing but like a contact. So very you make a contact and get it to release it. So has the living also looks like this? It makes like this. It releases like this. It makes like this. Delicious like this. And it takes a very short do that. So 20 milliseconds sufficient for the buttons. Now there will not be any repeat execution also because now even after the switch becomes higher, it will wait for 20 milliseconds before executing exiting this condition, which is enough for the demands to execute. These are the core fundamentals of accepting a digital input on any microcontroller overall in your system. So I want you to experiment with everything in detail. Digital. Now, see, I'm going to press the switch. And I'm going to release it now. No matter how you press it and how you release it. You will not see a double exclusion switch to, if you remember, last stance, which was given almost always a double execution that is inherent in the nature of the beast, which is that to is indeed a mechanical conduct. So a mechanical contact will never be made like instantly, never been released instantly. They will always play like this. And therefore we have added this demands to never, ever, ever. You will see that there is any kind of response now. So this is all for now. This is what you can see as the fundamental of accepting that digital inputs on iOS. And not only yes, we totally do, but basically every other microcontroller.

# PRACTICE TASKS WITH DIGITAL INPUT ON ESP32

Hi. Now that we have seen the sample program with Switch, I have few tasks for you to execute. I'm going to show you one of them. And I would like you to execute some of them, either one of them using your own practice. Actually, there are a number of different tasks, which I would just add. So what I want you to do is create an app. Don't this and switch then a simple entity control using switch the two elements and dosages. Then one switch. It's pressed both on and when. And then switch is both again to erase and to switches. And this time, what I want you to do is I want you to do a little control on individual switches. When one switch is pressed and ready one on, then the other switches pressed and it is one off and. And you do two on. So these are some basic tasks I would like you to do with sutures. Okay. I'll just show you this tool so that you get an idea of how to do that. And then you can continue with the other things.

## Tasks Based on Switch

- Up Down Counter using switch
- LED Control using switch
- 2 LEDs and 2 switches. When one switch is pressed, both ON and when other switch is pressed both OFF
- 2 LEDs and 2 switches. When one switch is pressed, LED2 OFF and LED1 ON when another switch is pressed LED1 OFF and LED2 ON

So I've done control using switch. First of all, let us copy this entire code. Take it into a new folder or new sketch. And then save it as a down counter switch. Now what I do here is along with this to switch once this to liquidation, I live near a variable called college, which by default is zero.

very well till now. So Ipswich one expressed what I will do. It's. Count clusters. Cyril, the French count equal to then Lord Byron Ellen Count and

Delia Thompson. So the count will be incremented and will be printed on the serial port and the of thousand resistance. Similarly, we will do it from minus. The only thing we have to make sure about minus is you don't want to see values. Then you do. So I'll just do this. If count is less than zero counted. Zero. This is a single line. If condition. Therefore, you can skip the limit. Remember, if there are multiple lines and if condition, then you have to have the opening entries. But if it is a single condition, you can skip that. So my program is done. Let's see the output. So I will upload it into the system now and we'll try to see. Again. It will see here. It's important. You don't want all the counts to be implemented by two times in a single switch. So you may want to add the pulling effect to you. It's called it's pulling when you on purpose, stall the microcontroller. Stop the microcontroller from doing other things. It's only. I have not done any polling here. So let's see, because I have Ed 1/2, which is usually sufficient to move my finger on the switch. Now I clicked it once and found this one. I click it another thing. Counties to actually get one more thing down the street. Now I'm a little bit pressed, so if I came in president with a delay of 1/2, the count will keep incrementing. See released nine Prestwich to become6543217.

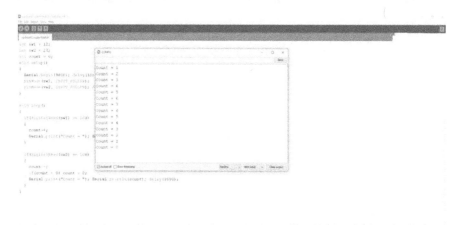

After that, it might have gone into the negative headlines, but it won't because now we have redone it that if it was less than zero, then the conceivable. And then you can increment it like this. Now, this is just one example. In the same way you can have an LCD declared, make it on here, make it off here, make it. Any number of GPI goes on and off in this if conditions off switch for this. You can also make something like if digital switch 1% and 4%. If digital data switched to just like that, you can mix and match those conditions. But for this session, I will not add those complexities because I don't want you to be scared about it in the percentage. So this is the basic switch interface. I hope you will be able to do this. The sites. Please try to follow the bread tutorial that I'm going to add into the section. Please remember this tutorial projects for breadboard are not different from. They were shot almost ten years ago, but they are. I think this should be sufficient for you to get an idea of how to interface with the breadboard. If you already know about the breadboard, then you skip the projects. But if much. There is nothing to. There is no harm in deflation. Some of the knowledge that's about it for this project, guys, trying to do these exercises and let meknow if you face any issues. Thank you.

# RELAY SWITCHING CIRCUIT INTERFACING WITH ESP32

Hi. Now let's try to understand how we can perform. The switching off includes our items to exclude things becomes most interesting because this is nota real application. Then look, maybe you want to turn on. Let's see, life skill from which you have any of is going to see an experimental mode. Let's say you want to turn on fat, you want to turn on appliances. Most of the household appliances that you see are operating on insurance. Depending upon where you are, we may have utility world 50 hertz. Our hundred and ten volt. 60 hertz on a 50 hertz leg that supply. I'm not going into the basics of this because I'm assuming that you know something about what kind of pieces of now you have, but when you have easy supply to switch or when you have a supply on which you want to turn on your device, then this kind of transistor switch. And so it will just not work at all because the transistor is an active device first thing. It will definitely not work at all with these two circuits. Second thing is there is no isolation here from the microcontrollers like H2, transistor and load.

So first thing is it will not work at all, that's for sure. And other. We can't use that because if we do, then the microcontroller circuits damaged due to the AC mortgage. So we need a different kind of circuitry in order to interface inside devices or in order to turn on an office in devices with a microcontroller making it better to do what would be the kind of circuit that would then create or what do we use? Let's. So what do we use for this purpose? It's something called this really is a very old and most widely used device for easy device switching. The nature of it such that it just doesn't matter with the units. AC Or which is just that because the really works to me like a mechanical switch. It is very suitable for AC. Let's, let's see how the really construction is and how we can turn on it. So really usually consist of a coin iPad sports let's say L1 L2 depending upon which symbol you refer. The point means may be different. Some might call it a, B, some excellent. It can see once in one day what it can. So it does consist of an electromagnetic pulse. And then there is a magnetic coupling and sort of that magnetic coupling. What I'll do is just show you like this. So there are terminals, three different terminals to this, really. What is Calder's legacy? And one as follows Look and see. The third one is called It's Common. The construction is very simple. Let me show you how it works. So there is a small spring attached to the this terminal, which gives it connected. And all the little all the time it's connected to. And then the related script on a table. Then the release of it is followed of there is no material. Then the exhibition and the comment is going to and you'll see this spring pull up. Now what happens is when you give a little will attach to L1, there is no polarity to it. You can give here positive negative here or negative here and positive here. And there is a return voltage for let's say it's a 12. 34 divided by like that. Let's see if we have a 12 volt coin and let's see if I give 12 volt across this. Two points being a complete vesicle. What happens is the Colgate's magnetized because of the magnetism that is induced in the point the common terminal it's attracted or pulling against this string tension. And now this connection is broken and the common is not connected to. How long it happens. As long as you have kept the dual world supply given to the economy, as long as the supply is energized, government will be connected to. When you remove this exhibition and you remove the voltage applied across, we're not fences, the magnetism dies down and the ball again goes back on. The common amine goes back to. And. So the really it's switched onto the common it's connected to end that is normally open then you give supply to the reelected. If you don't then the common good is going to be to and. Now because of this. What happens is let's say I want to perform a switching circuit. So in the typical switching circuit, what I do is next to this is my is this supply and this is my light switch, which I usually want to do. And this is my load. It can be any type of tube, light bulb, whatever you want to connect with it. Now, when you press the switch, when you make this mark that the Lord runs on and then you release the content, the Lord turns off the. So it becomes interesting when you use it in a very simple way that this one terminal will be your end and the other terminal will become. So when you turn on the dealer by giving supply word bids across, what will happen? It's the end of Anchorman. We get started with each of them. There is literally a mechanical contact. There is a sound of the. And the lawyer will tell. When you remove the excitation voltage, the load will turn off. That's simple as that. I'll also try to create a computer circuit for it so that we can remember it very well. I'm going to keep this for now. Now let me open is the idea that I'm going to use to create the circuits and I will show you how the same can be done. Now, look at this. This is how a typical relay symbol will look like. Forget about the part numbers. This is how it will look like. So there are two points to which we call this coin. We have the supply and then you can see there are three terminals. Now, as you can see here, the number one and five are connected to each of them. So I can denote them as a lot.

relay coil voltage
U3
SRU-05VDC-SL-C

And this one is another. And this one is. And so this one is. This one is noisy and this one's coming. Let's see. Let's go and see. Look, Scarlett. I know. Okay. Now when you have this kind of configuration switching circuits. Or the actual roadside circuit. Will be like that. So let me see if I have an easy supply source of. Solet's see if I get an alternative. An AC source. Let's just follow them as the source. Look, stick a bulb, for example. Any kind of will do. Actually, this is just a symbolic representation that we're going to have. Now, Drew. Don, let's do this bulk and do not this using this let's not call it ultimatum, but with ACS applied, the configuration will go like this. So this point, one point of law will get connected to the supply. Other point of the supply. There is no plus minus actually to see the movement. So NC study one of the two determinants of coming in and will go to supply. And the other one. You go to the other point of, look, this is how you will connect to your lord across the aisle in order to turn it on and off. And now the biggest question is if the Lord works on blustering world, how can we give this to involve American troops? We simply just cannot. So how this really will turn on using microcontrollers here as a microcontroller. So the answer, short answer is no. You cannot directly turn on the law or you cannot directly turn on the relay using microcontroller alone. Then what will you do? The answer was that in the previous project itself, you can use or you can tweak this coin as you see load. And what you can do is you can use an MP and transistor over here. So one point of law will go to trial. The second point will go to base of transistor collector of transistor emitter of transistor available to ground and towards the base. We connect equipment three water supply and give this to any kind of microcontroller, which is a GPIO. Like that, and this value can be prepared. So this is how you complete the illicit use of it will come into the picture. Now, there is one sharp, tiny problem with this kind of circuit. Just a moment. And the problem is because. Used to call it trouble because the delinquent is in it when father son, a good Samaritans extorts charges. But when you let's say you make this in zero, then what will happen? The stored charges are not going in, and therefore the relay may be turned on or may steepened on for one. So you need some kind of prediction circuits for this really to switch off. And that prediction circuits that can come in the form of a dial. So what we need to do is connect the dial in reverse class ambition of the US mass population across the planet. So the content of the art should go to Squid ward. Now, because of that, what happens is when you turn on the relay, the diet is not a picture at all. It is totally reverse fast. But when you switch it off, when you make the spin zero, what happens is the junctions are not button bars. They are reversed less. So the connection from this point towards zone is broken. Now what happens because of this four charges into this really point, the polarities of this relate to us. And it gives a conducting plot to desire in itself for the charges to get released and quickly within. 100 or 200 milliseconds at the max, the relic when it's discharged and even hundred. If it is a good time missing, it quickly gets discharged and immediately see the relay being turned off. Now, apart from that, some may also want. My job is to give you everything that might be needed. Maybe you're creating an industrial project. Apart from that, some also want to have LSD as an indication of the rules being turned on or not. So you can connect and be like this. This is totally optional. Okay, this circuit that I'm giving here, it's totally optional. It's not mandatory at all. But if you're going to do something like this, what happens is the entity will turn on along with the relevant. And so when you make this bill one the announcement on the device will turn on and this and individuals that are not giving that indication just to make sure that it doesn't get as much current use this as high value that this stuff. Very one of the really the start of giving you an indication this diode acts as a prediction circuit for it and this is how it computes your entire circuit. Now let us continue this far into our presentation for you. Obviously the reference of it will not work like that. So do these and use the snippets of tool. And I will do this in. Not looking that good. Just a moment. So we just. It's the same thing here. Let's just assume it a bit.

Let's turn off the grid. Now. It's good to. Copy into the presentation. Well, I hope this thing is clear with you. Now, the next question is, how do you actually make this kind of connection? Either we can make this kind of connection on your own, or you can also refer to the readily available reading audience. I opened one. I'm just going to show you one. There are many different vendors from whom you can purchase this thing. But let me show you one. So in India it's something I prefer to buy from. So you get five volt or you get one channel. Really, if you look at it closely, you can see there are those three transistors for the ladies and transistor and the other reality for switching. Then there is a small switch and I can see and it is a small transistor also really, and the three terminals sticking out. Now, if it were the relay, the coil would be just five words. So you need to unify all that supply here. Input with the signal coming from controller and as the ground supply of controller. If you're good on the relay, then expand to six people. Then have your party this. This is the current rating of you. When you are collecting laws like this, do you really again, you have to take into account how much you currently have. Nobody is going to take and depending upon how much load it takes, you might change that element of you using readily available. You get a single channel and you get the dual channel relay. Now this generally also comes with an optical so that whatever switching circuits you connect or here it has no effect on the microcontroller. The signal is optically isolated. So here are the grounds that are not very common with the illegal. So you get different types of circuits and different type of laws, as you can see here. So depending upon what is your requirement, you may use any such type of signal channel module, multi-channel module, even you get for the channel relay itself. Really, you also get a higher cut in the modules to be. You can see there are eight channel animals also for the channel. Also, it's all based upon your requirements. I hope it clarifies the concepts of the switching and the next module type of connecting is similar actually.

# RELAY SWITCHING CIRCUIT WITH ESP32 – 2

Hi. Now that we have tried to understand the theory behind intricacy in the really. Now let's try to see some of it in action. So I'm following this exact schematic over here that translates to messaging. So it is created onto this interesting board, if you can see. So here we have a transistor, then a small in addition to the store combo. Then there is an additional instrument you can see which is going to the base of transistor. Then here I have really and here is a terminal which is the return and C command. And so the one beneath the red is gone and the rightmost one. And as you can see, I'm following this exact circuit over here. If you can see here, then this is a tube in a C cable. If I just show it to you completely. So this is my. A cable. And here one point of the cable.

# Relay Switching Circuit

As you can see in the schematic is going to the relay contact here. The other point of the relay contact, it's going to. But this is the bulb. Okay. And the other point of the bulb is then going to. The AC cable itself. So AC these are the two points of one point of the going to really other point of delivering the AC cable. And the other point, obviously cable going back to exactly what we have seen here. And I also happen to have a bulb connected to this. I have connected this spin over here. Which has been a virtual arrangement to the base of Transistor. And a very simple, little blinking program. It's in action. Now, let's see the requirements to involve one which is provided on this supply. If you don't have this one or if you don't have any such kind of interests involved, then you can easily obtain the readily available related to this box which comes in markets. Let me show you that in a moment. Logic and see here, this is a single module. Something like this will be easily available in local markets. Focus. So it has got a 12 volt input line. Then this input this should be coming from microcontroller and this is the granted. So this is a single channel really model. I'll give you the same thing here. You can see an order them here and set it down here. The middle one is onwards and then the similar base. You may also find a two channel delay module for the channel delay module on any system. The logic underlying logic remains the same. Now, what I've done is I have simply used a small blinking program on the budget. If you look at the code here now, let's try to download this code and then. Let's see the output. When the code is downloaded, you can also start hitting the pixel three. I'm not sure if that will be audible from this distance of microphone, but let's see now. The code has been compiled. And it's uploaded. Now the program has been uploaded into the. Bold. Now. Let's see if it works. Now, if you see here's this spot power indication, it's on off. And I'm going to stick my microphone near to the rear. You may hear the sound of picking clear my name, but it not coming on off, however. Let's make some changes. It's not that long ago. It's nothing. You have to remember very well that it's this line of life going to be here. So if you are quoting you all the above, make sure you do not touch anything over here. And before I want to do is I just use the in 60 seconds. Once it gets too fast off switch immediately. When it comes to switching plugs, the might sometimes give them for the purpose of simplicity and also using a small delta so that all these sort of innovations can be carried out very easy.

We are also planning to switch the symbol on and off to Alexa. So the circuits and my setup is going to remain the same. Now I'm going to connect this to main spot supply and I'm going to start. So that as you can see with the reliance on. You have the audible feedback from here. But it is all. Getting it. Now I'll take the microphone back to my column that it should belong. Really? Just a moment. Okay.

Now, this is my in transit as it looks like. Now one thing is here, I'm using external power supply, 12 volt power on this into this board. So you also have to make sure the ground of is Win32 and this socket is very common, as you can see through this green line. Anyhow, if you are interfacing a board, a small signal memory like this, then it will have coiled voltage. Right then inputs and the ground builds. So here. Because. The ground should be made of common materials that have to do ground as well as transport. And they should be coming from controllers. I would stay here with you. We will be using the same setup. Maybe we will have some other prints, but we're using the same setup whenever we are experimenting with triplets.

# READING CAPACITIVE TOUCH INPUTS ON ESP32

Hi. In this project, we'll try to see how we can see on how we can utilize the capacitive touch screens on iOS. We touch ID, you can use them to turn on or off any particular load, or you can also use them as switch inputs. Instead of applying or using physical buttons, you can use them as menu buttons for identity and you can use them for. Any such proposals. Okay. So for this experiment, all I'm going to have is a single ESD 32 federal 32 board. Basically, this is an absolute was up in the 32 board, which is based on USP 32 and I'm going to use a single pin. Female Two female connectors over here. So it has got. Female So the male two male connectors because what we connect on one inch as well as on the other and on the softer side, I'm going to use the E and I'm going to use another software to make it interesting, which is called S terminal by the. C-Terminal by Brie. This is interesting. Yes, of project, Arduino has a built in serial monitor, but I just want to see things in a different way. That's why I'm asking you to download this software. It's a very simple utility. I'm going to chart single file that you can download and start to use. This is basically the serial terminal replacements. So usually on a development computer, this it's so useful utility that I keep it on my desktop almost all the. So this is terminal. We are going to use this for what? I'll show you. Meanwhile, let's get back to. We told you. So with this photo, if you look at the pin now, we have so many touch inputs that that's zero, that's six, nine, that's three, that's aged at 70 my vegetables. So all in all, the number 1432, 15, 33, 27, 12, 13 and then before, these are the touch inputs which we have on the industrial tools output due to board.

## How to accept capacitive touch on esp32 Feather Board (touchread)

- 14
- 32
- 15
- 33
- 27
- 12
- 13
- 4

Now if you have to use any of them, all you need to do is simply use a function called touch you. How does this function looks like to see that? First of all, I just took a blank sketch. Let's do a wild setup. And definitely we can also be doing what we do and saying to score adds capacitive touch inputs. Let's begin. Zero. Zero. And here what I'm going to do is let's stick a project of Alexa in the call to Dutch attitude and just give up in them. So we have all indispensable connections, like CEOs. Say, pin number 14 on the board in number 14 is here. So that's already been number 14 cereal. Don't put in an egg and then you stick a small do you. Okay. Thousand millisecond so that we have some time duration between two inputs. Now if you look at it carefully, I'm not sure whether it focuses well or not, but this it's a C, I and this is been number for. So I have been number 14 over here, to which I'm connecting a single wire. Okay. What's the problem here? Let me look at my coach. Okay. It has not got any collusive tax on capital here. So let's upload it again. Meanwhile, I have this one wire over here, as you can see, connected to pin number four pin. After the code is downloaded, we will open the cereal terminal and will try to attach this particular flash with you. And we needed to know what is the difference between the different touches that we may have. Remember, when everything is in capacitive touch input like this, you will have to estimate the same manner that I'm doing. Legacy when nothing is trashed here. The value that is coming on the Syrian port, it's 62, 63, something like that. Now I'm going to just gently give it a touch. I touched it and you see the value dropped down to 31 something. I raised my finger. 64, 64, 64, something that's stuck in the velodrome stop. Okay. So 64 AIDS or about 60, it's something that you don't touch. And below 40, it's something you touch. See here. As simple as that. So the testing is done so easily. Why? I wanted to ask if we just should. Okay. We don't do the software. We have a serial plotter here also in our dinners. So I'm just wanting to have a little fun here. I'm not going to give any delay. So what will happen is will get data very fast, but I'm still terminal and I want to plot them. So I showed you about Terminal by Billy, but it's okay if you don't download that because we have a serial slaughtering tools also since usually I used to use the terminal, maybe we show you that softer as well after this one step. Now the touch is being read and send on the input first. This is really. So if I just open serial plotter, you'll see these are the values we're getting them continuously. Now, if I touch it. See. That's it. That's it. That's it. It's very easily visualizing. The Syrian border is moving dynamically very fast. So I'll just stop. Serial plotter. And since we have downloaded, let's do this. So the company we have, it's content. And what we want to do is we want to simply create a graph. Now let's connect. For some reason. It just crashed just a moment ago. Okay. It's up to this question. Nevertheless, I hope you got the idea over here with serial plots. So if I catch. Even the Bible is in my hand, because if I touch even the blood from outside, that is supposed to do that. As you can see. Okay. Now, I'll just keep it like this the way it is now here on the breadboard. It's just a gentle touch. And the valuable strong. Now, if you want to turn on or off or devices and things, then just do watch more. In addition to school built in, come off outputs here instead of even serially printing it. What I do is. If it is less than 40 and digital ride quality and also built in common higher health and digital lives and the d underscore built in coma it wins.

What if the if the touch input that is delayed or recorded is less than 40 then. I want to turn the LCD on otherwise and it should be turned off. Now let's try to see this in action. So he and I have. Code is been downloaded. I think it's done. Now that's the spirit. And you see that the difference is noticeable. Just let's stick it to you. Dutch. Dutch, Dutch. At Symbolisms. Now in this way you can use all the available touch inputs on iOS with touch ID. What are the other inputs available to you? You have all this and personally, at least on the Fed that are due to world. If you have any other use 52 compatible balls then it may have more for us. We have one, two, three, four, five, six, seven, eight prints over here which can be used as touch inputs.

# DHT22 SENSOR INTERFACING WITH ESP32

Hi. In this project, let's start to see some actual sensor interfacing with ISP such as, you know, the primary purpose, primary motive of disproject is to learn Internet of Things or IAG applications and therefore having sensor values which we can sense or intermarriage or to some other place is a vital part of disproject. Let's start now. There are different types of sensors available and depending upon how much you have already done in embedded systems, you can correlate with this things. Although I'll give a perspective of a compute pressures. If you have some experience, then you are easily able to understand and even give you a couple of depressions. It's particularly for you, but don't worry. So there are basically two type of sensors which you went to visit microcontrollers. One is called as an analog sensor, which can view a specified voltage, which relates to the applied analog input. For example, there is a temperature sensor called 1135 which gives an millivolts 30 degrees Celsius. So if my room temperature currently is 25 degrees Celsius, it will give an output of 50 me which to interface microcontroller with this kind of sensors. What we need is to use an E to convert an analog to digital converter which can convert this value into a particular digital output, which then can be used to understand the sensor value and perform the relative or required operations based on which. Then there are digital sensors. Digital sensors also come in different types, and the most popular or the most simplest one is something called that's of very basic one zero output sensor. So I will not be covering the sensors because they are pretty straightforward to use. So there can be a fired sensor, there can be a sound sensor, there can be any such kind of sensor which does that. It gives an output of logic. One when they send something or output of logic zero and they don't send some to be. Air sensor is also one such thing which can be used to detect the presence of a human body inside a room or something like that. And then comes. The most interesting part was the sensors, which gives digital data over some kind of protocol. Maybe they give you data on protocols like IPC, or maybe they give you data in terms of the rate of the signal, like ultrasonic sensors and others are going to send some sense of it. You spit out you. Now for the scope of this project, I am particularly not going to cover the analog inputs and it is a reason for which I hope you will be able to relate with that. And the reason is the analog input. Obviously 32 are not that well documented. You will be disturbed, you will be confused by looking at a lot of different tutorials online. So some of them will see it will read from 0 to 3. 3, some of them will see it will read from 0 to 1. 1volt. And most importantly, even if you figured out all the documentations and understand how to use it, the end result is the easy to do to analog. It spins up nonlinear so you will not be able to differentiate between different digits. Very remote. It is okay to use analog input for academic projects or just for the studies case, but that's out of the scope of this project. I want you to understand this better to do and start computing industrial grade project as well. So my ideal suggestion is if you all want to use an analog input, then please go and use some the external in this picture for the scope of this project. I'm not going to include analog voltages, but I will keep adding different projects on use with what you do in the project as well as on the YouTube channel, which will showcase how we can interface with different sensors now. But in the scope of this project, I'm going to use the HD to do temperature and humidity sensor. The reason being first, it is very easy to interface with DSP. And the second thing is it is very easily available across the world. It is cheaper and we usually get it. Almost every is modular. If you look at the popularity of the institute, you can see the official tutorials of provided by Microsoft, Azure and Amazon. This also includes this one sensor with controller which can demonstrate the details sending onto the cloud. So let's try to understand the Institute for this use.

# DHT22

Interfacing with ESP32

So I have this two sensors with me currently. One is called DSD two and the blue one, which you can see here. It's called SDH two. And it is I'm just going to show this to you for comparison. So the issue two looks like this white big one, and the B is two. And when it's smaller, usually we don't use the estimate of an audience because it is not so accurate. The range of sensing is also not so good and therefore these 2 to 2, it's kind of the standard thing to use. Now how you can use the issue to do, let's try to understand some basic specifications first. So it has a very wide operating temperature range out of the sensing range. I would see that it's from -40 degrees Celsius. It can zero 200% of humidity. It works on 3 to 6 volt operating voltage and it has a very good resolution of the reading defense. Moreover, the connection of the issue to two is also very simple. If you look at it, this is actually a module. Okay, so the sensor itself is a four wire sensor. As you can see over here in this image, it looks focused. Not now, me. So it looks like this. Which has got to be number one, two, three, four. Then number one is sick. And number two is data three is not connected.

# DHT22 Pinout

- Pin 1 → 3.3v
- Pin 2 → GPIO with 10k Pullup
- Pin 3 → NC
- Pin 4 → GND

And for this count, the number two, that is data. It can go to any of the three to you and get pulled up. So the schematic, if you want it, should be looking like this. If you get just the sense this one, then you need to create a schematic like this. But what I have here is a module. Now let me just get closer to it so we can focus it. So on the model, if you check, focus. You can see there are only three points ground zero and data and the required full up resistor is all readily available. With you. So depending upon if you're getting a module or if you are getting a particular sensor directly, the sensor Texel you have to choose which you want to go for. Now, let me make the connections first so that it becomes easier for us to start experimenting. So here I inserted into the Mississippian the attainment. And I'm going to connect it to. 3. 3. So I have some. Male to male. Female to male bias here to make my life easier.

And I connected it to 2. 3% or not. I'm going to use another combination of male female to create a larger wire. And this one I will use as the tap in. I'm going to connect the deep up into I'm going to really connect it to energy by you. But I'm particularly using the spin a lot. So it's the ACL fault in. So to do so, just leave me connected to working. Basically it doesn't matter actually that you connected so they could be number 40 and I'm connecting it to. No. I mean, so it is a seal and steer seal in this. It's forbidden. And lastly, I want to connect account here. So make sure when you are using devices or connections, then try to keep your writing simple so that you can understand which. I don't have much good advice here. As a luxury much of my body is to do to since it is not connected. Once you have the issue to two connected. All you need to do is to install some libraries in order to get to the sensor and display the values on. That's what we are going to do now. So the two libraries you're going to need is to send celebrity by the throat and a unified sensibility. Now, let's. Let's test the waters. So let's open our Dino. And here, let me just stick a new sketch. Completely new one. And I will save it as the HD to do. Yes. I'm just going to call it as the institute est and let's try to see the output of which first of all, do auto sketch include liability and manage litigants. Here, you will have to search for the celebrities with jobs to do so. One of the best is in celebrity by the fruit and fruit universe and celebrity. So the HD, I just type HD and look at all the BSD related libraries available. As a

71

part of experimentation, you are free to use any of the libraries also. I'm going to use a of libraries because I am using data from smaller. So this is the issue isn't celebrity married approach. Just install. Nothing. It is also asking you that it depends on unified sense of liability. So better if we have a chat itself and all. So we have installed the BSD as well as any parts and celebrity. Now simply go to find. Examples. Here you will find the installed library. So enough root beer stews and celebrity. Unless Sydney is stupid. Now I'm going to complete this score completely over here in my test score. Let's simplify things a bit. Okay. Let me just remove the unwanted comment first. So that becomes easier for us to understand. You can anyways go to the documentation later on. So this is the step in and this is the history type. And then there are just the values being read. Each is humidity followed by its temperature. I don't want any of the stuff coming in here and just want to print it. Okay, so let's keep it simple. So humidity is X percentage and then temperature, it's the next degree Celsius. Nothing else that we want to keep. Index. Nothing. Nothing. Nothing. And let's just have a of those events. So it was already there in the beginning of the call. So all we need to do is download this score where I have connected the distances that I just need to mention that number. So it is. For billion, for sure. So let's put the strap in to be one for Ambien, then. So you can really function here. All we have is this tool functions which will enable us to read the temperature as well as humidity from the sensor. So let's try to upload this code now and see the object. The code is being compiled. Sometimes you may get impatient sometimes about the operating of. How did the downloading process with you is with attitudes a little bit definitely slower as compared to the regularity the books. Now the completion is almost about to be done and we'll start uploading the code into the board and then we'll be able to see the output. Exploring now. Connecting, writing and acting, writing. Directing. Done. It's possible, but. Nothing. It is not able to do anything. You need to be prepared with this also. Now, this is a problem and I am not going to commit to this moment. I'm not going to edit this with you because this is going to happen with most of us. We cannot to be too sensitive for the first time. We may not get the output correctly. We may get something wrong. Something is mistaken. So what do you have to do here is you have to check for the power cables correctly and then also checkthe data being been connected correctly. Also, I have Mr. French a new line here, so I will do that. And meanwhile, I'll keep checking, dividing. Now, as you can see now, I have made some changes. Okay. Identically installed the sensor on the board. And just that it's some visual library, which I'm not able to connect to the screen very well. So what I've done is I'm using PIN number 27 now, and now I can see the output. Now, this is a very simple experiment. You can also try to increase the humidity by doing something they put on to it. If you can see the humidity increase to 78, 83. If you do and the temperature is the temperature is basically the room temperature. If I have no small and so it let's see if it changes the temperature of it. Not much change the impression, I would say, but my camera lens is a little bit cheaper because itis on for some time. So let me touch it with the camera and let me see if I can notice some change, some sensing elements inside. So you will have to have heart it going through this. So therefore it is a very perfect candidate for sensing the room temperature and humidity inside your house. So this is the institute. So you might want to make changes according to your core. Now I'm connecting it here on V number 27 and now the breadboard connection between the seven is looking. But also my sense it is a bit old. Maybe it was not connecting well with the wires, so I have directly mounted it on to the bridge. Now this is how you can get the humidity and temperature values to be a strict sensor. But this is just the start of or beginning of the stored. Similarly, there can be a number of different sensors which can be used. So this is a very simple sound sensor.

```
// - DHT Sensor Library: https://github.com/adafruit/DHT-sensor-library
// - Adafruit Unified Sensor Lib. https://github.com/adafruit/Adafruit_Sensor

#include "DHT.h"

#define DHTPIN 14      // Digital pin connected to the DHT sensor

#define DHTTYPE DHT22  // DHT 22  (AM2302), AM2321

DHT dht(DHTPIN, DHTTYPE);

void setup() {
  Serial.begin(9600);
  Serial.println("DHTxx test!");

  dht.begin();
}

void loop() {
  // Wait a few seconds between measurements.
  delay(2000);
  float h = dht.readHumidity();
  float t = dht.readTemperature();
  Serial.print("Humidity: ");
  Serial.print(h);
  Serial.print("%  Temperature: ");
  Serial.print(t);
  Serial.print("°C ");
}
```

As I said, it simply gives logical one or zero. And this is a proximity sensor. It gives one output logic, one of logic zero whenever you put the hand in front of it. And then there are a number of different sensors which can be used to get different values. What we are going to do is we are going to give you setups on one is the 2 to 2 sensor and the other one is this are able and using this two setups, we will be performing a number of different experiments that are related to . So that's about it for this project. Trying to do DSD due to interfacing your cell and see this code works for you.

# ESP32 WIFI BASED DEVICE CONTROL

Hey, in this project, we'll see how we can perform device control over easy to do using the home my family took. Remember this experiment of this practice that I show you does not require any active internet connection. And if you just have a single modify router, that's all you need. So let's see what is the concept and what we are trying to do here? The concept is very simple. What we're going to do is we are going to connect the yes, we touch it to a relay module just like we have seen multiple times before. And then now we're are going to connect to ease. We touch to do for the first time to the network, that is to the Wi-Fi, which is the major purpose of using your strategy. 32 And all we are going to connect to use for to do all of us to find network and a simple program return on genius. We will convert the 32 into a kind of it should be so awesome you can see a very mini on a micro level it should be solar which cancer and its general page. The workflow will be very simple. So once you use be 32, it's connected to your home life and a took it will act as a solar. So whatever device is connected to a network, it will get an IP address and this IP address can be accessed through any other device like phone or laptop connected to the same home life character. And you can open a browser here, put the IP address of Yes, you touch you too and you will see a page in the browser over here. That page will give you commands or action to turn something on or off, or to turn a particular relay or entity on or off on the hospital. We are creating a demonstration circuit off of the unit here, but I think you get the idea. If you can turn on the you know, you can turn on and off almost anything you want. So in short is for you to access. And some of you can see a very small webpage.

# Wifi Device Control

- Esp32 acts as a mini http server
- Serves a small web page
- You can take actions in this page
- Relay / LED Control

You can take actions on this page and in turn you can perform the relay of control in order to perform this experiment on our table using SD 32. What we need to is we are going to need a particular level two particular attributes which needs to be manually installed. Remember the libraries we have used before, they were all installed automatically using the library manager. But here the libraries are going to be admitted to manually installed as well as the schematic parties. Consent schematic is the same one. We are using an approach vendor who supported you as you must have known till now, and we have it in this switching socket just like which has been shown over here exactly same, no change at all. And we have a few suppliers. The list of connected with you. The two libraries which are required are actually embedded in this presentation also. And I have also given you the links for both of them. The library installation, it's actually very simple. So this is, let's say, a zip file that you will download, for example, from the link that I have provided. So extract the zip file. What happens is. You look at a folder like this. This folder will have a folder in which all the lives of this unpleasant. All you need to do is copy this folder. So there are two libraries. One is CSP asynchronous server, and another one is async DC. All you need to do is let me show you batch as well. So this one it is extract to the stop. I'll show you both of them how it works. So we have nothing to see here. And is a symptom of sort of us. Remember, don't keep the library as if it's like this. You have to use the folder which is inside of it. So I'll just take that folder out here. And left everything else. So these are the two libraries which we need to install. How? Lucy? Just copy the two folders. And then go to a computer, go to the location that article is installed, which is in program files except six Arduino. And here you'll find a political liability. If you look at here, that is a political liabilities. This is the old method of installing libraries before there was left to manage. So simply put these two folders over here and now you can run the code provided. So let me show you the score for now. I would suggest you do not go into the details of this score. Okay. You can very well just use this score as a dance for now. And then you may try to make changes according to what you teach. For now, let me show you what of the changes that I'm doing here. So I'm going to use only one really therefore has defined number relates. This one barometer is only one. And I'm correcting that a little bit. But you can look at my schematic over here. My release is connected with GPI. Therefore, I'm writing on this one. If you want multiple number of arenas, just Ed and add those numbers over here. So without any of further changes or delays, let's try to upload this code onto the controller and see the output. So I'm starting to upload here and I'll be explaining you the pluses for taking note. So once you have done everything at such a state, all you need to do is you have to insert your life credentials into the program. So let's let me show it to you here. I'm currently inserting my life with initials over here, and you have to do this, then get your credentials. Okay, so this is something I use. I am not hiding it at all because frankly, I'm not letting you come into my home to steal the iPhone out, for that matter, anything. So this is my life it to ensure that I use this as a society. This is a unit to replace the students according to what you are using. After you replace the credential, upload the code, opens it in terminal with about rate of man 600check IP address assigned to EESP 32 and open that address on phone or computer. Let me add one more step here. This in the iOS 52, after you open the seal, tell me this, because sometimes what happens, you already uploaded the code and now if you start it, it will start from the beginning, from the scratch. So let's change the voltage to 9700. I will keep my camera open over here. So it gives a better idea what is happening. Okay. And now I'm going to push research on my. Is it you?

Now as the research it is trying to connect to the next one, connecting to one. And now we got an IP address. Now there are two ways to do it. Let us see the one way, which I guess most of you will like that is using on a mobile phone. So what I'll do is I'll just open the mobile phone browser over here. And the we enter the IP address, I guess you will be able to see that now. So it is. 1922. 168. 20. 1627. It's visible now. And now you can see I have got a page over here.

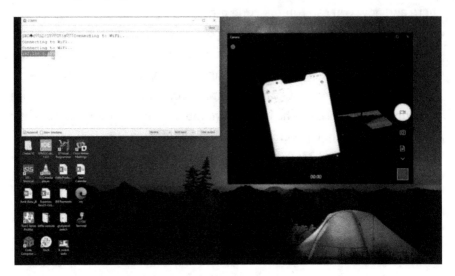

Maybe you're not able to see it completely because a lot of camera issues. Okay. But let me get to it here. It's not it's not visible. Well, now let's change it only to focus the phone. So there is a button here. On off on off button. But now that we have CMT for it, we try to open it on the computer screen. It's. I have all the connections made and now I'm also going to connect the AC cable, which will be useful to actually turn on or off the. And now. Let us open a process with some activity when you open Google Chrome, for example. I will keep it over here in a very small window. 1922. 168. 20. 167 IP address. You see it here and hit enter.

ESP Web Server

Now see web server apps that are done over here really number one go to. And you see the difference. I think you may have also heard the related. So I just making the switch on and off, on and off, on and off and then really it's starting. So this is my five best. Okay. You can use that on mobile. Let's say I'm now trying to use it on mobile also. Let's see if I can see the difference. You can use it on mobile. You can use it on laptop. You can use it almost anywhere. No, I have done it on my phone and it's off on PC. So even if a switch just now doesn't happen the meeting and now you can turn it off from because the original code is written by recycles of random tutorials and I have made changes to it to make it simplified bit more easier to understand. Now when you want to add more things, let me add another thing. That is the on chip. So that is that number 13. Then all you need to do is simply add those numbers over here into this curly bracket and then right number of rules as to, for example. And then in one setup program, all you need to do is you need to make sure you know the right set of billboards for the film deputies. That's all you have to use. If you want to experiment with more, if you want to do a little bit of, you know, do some exciting things or just make some changes into it, you can simply change this system in court, which has been served by this speech. This is the part of juvenile court. So I made changes to this each to hear. I made it in that proposal. 32. It's over. And now let's upload it again. Let me open my browser once again. So doesn't matter which one you use. 1922. 168. 0. 1627. That's the PS unit. But it's not changed yet because the code, it's still uploading, as you can see, or not even uploading it is only in the compiling stage itself for now. Now it's uploading was uploading is done. We will open the serial monitor. Almost immediately. Now it's connecting to a fire connected. We go to the same IP address and now they said this before the speech. Now you can see there are two different reliefs that is written over here, although one of them is actually delivered, one of them will be displayed somewhere around here. Okay. This is the switchboard, and we're going to turn it on. Okay. And now I'm going to turn it off. So this is happening over Wi-Fi. There is no cable connection. Of project there is a cable connection for power only and for downloading.

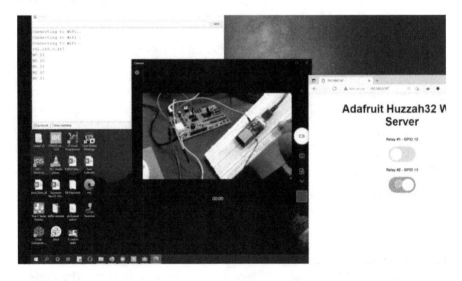

But it doesn't matters. It's working on fire. So this is my first. Really? This is my lady. You can see it here. This angle is good. Both of them are visible. First lamp of a lamp on the on. Lamp off, entity on. The only limitation with this kind of project. It's less a limitation, but it's walking on the lam x walking on the local network. You can also definitely go on and connect things to internet. What? The same phone will not work. When you want to control your devices over internet, it will be something else. It will be something different and what it will be. We will definitely be looking in upcoming projects. For now, I hope you must have liked this project. The code it's given to you and the schematic is given to you in the presentation itself. Triage on your own and see for yourself.

# ESP32 WEATHER MONITORING OVER WIFI (LAN)

Hi. In the last project, we have seen how we can perform a device control in the LAN. So I just thought of keeping this with you. Immediately after that, we do the weather monitoring using data in LAN, just like last project. Also, this project cord has been taken from random note audience. Please visit their website. They have quite a lot many different tutorials on use with a two on here. I have taken this code to make it simplified for all equals takers so that it should be easier for youto experiment on the Istituto and UC computer.

## Concept

The concept is completely similar. The only thing that has changed now is previously here we had a delay. Now here we have a new to 2%. So we have already understood about the issue to censor. It looks like this. It actually looks like it's just a forbidden connector. You can buy it as a model or as an individual sensor and you connect it to the. Yes, we touch it, too. Just like this. So pin number one should go to table number two is due to pin, which should go to image of go in in GPO 27. This data should look weird up to here. This is important because the output of this sensor, it's open, Jim. If it don't pull it up externally, it will not show any voltage levels, either one or zero. But that's an issue. Pull it up. It will get zero levels properly indicator when the battery is NC and the number four needs to connect to ground just like previous project in this one. Also, we need to add two libraries to already know since we have already read them. I will with that step and I'm pretty sure you have already seen the previous project. So we want to have this used to send celebrity matter fruit. We want to have the unified sense of library also. So all of these things are already done there. So I'm not going to repeat them over here. So let's directly open our camera and jumpstart into the action and see how this one goal works and what changes we can do in the and save this score. Does land issue to do with me? Open my camera here again.

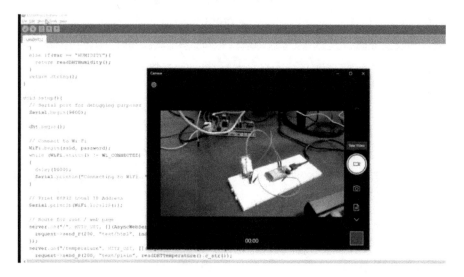

So as you can see, just to make things interesting, what I have done is I'm adding a certain amplitude, so I'm not going to touch it with soldering on, but I'll just keep it a bit close by so that I can blow some hot air into it. So if I keep it like this and if I. Alison Caldwell Alright then, I'm pretty sure that the issue will get a bit hotter. So the court is here again, the same changes. All you need to do is you need to just add your life insurance right over here. And then you need to mention the type of system that I'll just make to simplify and remove the unnecessary comment. So we have the issue to do connected to PIN number 27 and these are my last conventions, no other changes required for the schools. So let's upload this and see the output for this output. Also, we will either use a mobile browser or a computerized process. Let's. And the court had started compiling. And I know you know that it's it's quite slow, many of them. So let's wait here for some time. The uploading had started now. So let the record get uploaded completely and then will open the Syrian terminal that will see the IP address. Assange. Connecting to a fire. Connecting to a fire, connecting to find the IP. All we need to do again, just like last time it's copy this IP address. Open a browser and paste it over here. As you can see, there is a temperature and humidity value coming over here. But if I just try to do some experiment with just the. Gives. You can see the temperature is 27. 70. Refresh it. It's getting hotter. 21. Okay, so I have. Mm hmm. So this is the camera. This is what I'm doing here. So I'm just putting a heart.

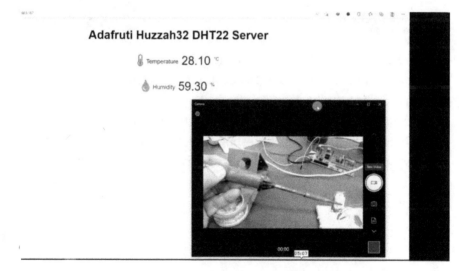

So then close to it, not touching it. Just closed, which. Okay. Make sure you if you do these exercises, be careful. Now you can see the temperature is 29. It is rising slowly. If I blow it, actually, it will reduce the temperature because of the cold air coming out of the smoke. If you have a hot air gun, it's much better. You can directly demonstrate. You can directly blossom some hot air over here. Unfortunately, I don't have one now, so I'm following something. We are vectors like this, but the points. I'm distraught, I guess. Every one of you. The temperature is rising. Am if I now kipyegon back in the counselor up to the sled with the salting gun holder, then you can see the temperature will start dropping now. 31. 60 then. Not much doubt. 31. 50. So on.

And so again, not to mention this time as well, what you can do is you can use a mobile browser also. But it's not visible. So we need to do it very dark in order for it to be okay. The fresh. 31. 2 refresh to 1. 1. 30. 9. So I have taken this two experience, particularly from an and I'm notorious and I thought they could be interesting to be added in the project maybe a study. So go to the projects about this or try to experiment onto the score, try to modify the code as much as possible and let me know how the experiment goes with you.

# ESP32 WEATHER MONITORING OVER WIFI (LAN)

Hi. Let's try to understand this code over here in this project, when you go step by step through all the lines in this little and will try to get an understanding of what this code is actually doing. So the very first thing is these are the libraries which are required for the web server, for the citizens of the school and for the wife to work this one. So these are the includes photos, Lebanon.

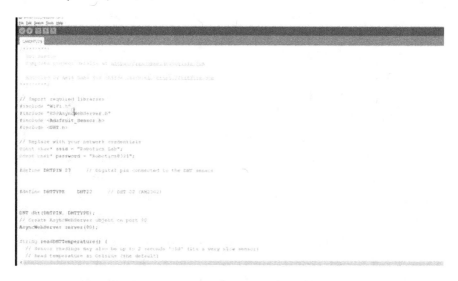

Then here is the network credentials. What they would want if I need to if you having you just need to mention the credentials with you try to use the 3 to 1 for me gigahertz only some if I have a 3. 2 gigahertz and five gigahertz dual mode. But try to use two one for the galaxy. Then here is the definition of where you're connecting the tapping of the external sensor. Here you define which sense of you use. It's a string to do on the one.

And then what we do here, it's in this line working, acting class. We are creating an object of the class. We. So the issue is celebrity, and we need to create an instance of this particular class by specifying the bin as well as the type of sensor. This DST over here is just a name given. Instead of this DHT, you can very well give your name a lot of my name over here. Similarly, we are creating a server instance over here. So the instance of us in Encrypts and what is created over here and the board member is specified as you know why it is because it is the default. But. If you want to have your website on any other report, then you have to specify that like this X, Y and z or WIPO to this and then it. So this it is by default. You want to if you don't mention anything like this, it is considered that it is 80. But if you want some other court like enslaves, it'll you can mention that over here. Then there is this string function which is reading the HD temperature and returning a string. Next, let the data type string for this function. Now what is done in this function is very simple. We are hitting the temperature into the variable called D and if there is any field read in this rating procedure, then the messages are logs on to the serial. I really disagree a lot. It's completely optional. It's just to give us an idea of the correct units that are coming. So there is no error or if there is an end, value is an end, is checking if the temperature and widths and an ideal and there is no such thing, then the print, the serial, the temperature, the time you all sit in terminal. So that's the function to do and pressure.

Similarly, there is a function to read geometry. Two different functions I mention.

You can, however, also have a single function, but then you'll have to go and do the pointers andall those things. So it's better to have two separate functions. Now here. Here we have a large score, which is actually the extension code for which because this is a large text, we don't want it to be stored in them, otherwise we will go out of the remedy. Therefore, the specified here its program, it means it will be stored in the flash memory, available in use, which is for. So therefore, this is or this is something that will be stored in the flash memory. If you want, you can just copy this whole text up to this line over here. So I don't want to completely delete that. I just want to see that copy that. You can see which in a notepad file and you can save your notepad file. As all files x, y, z dot estimate now x, y, z. It's stored as an extremely file. And you can see this is what that entire code is all about. So that code is basically this over here. Okay. Now that is the code for a statement stored in a variable. Then there is silly trivial function. Again, this is part of the same it's for. Up to this point. So this is entirely the extremely poor up to this overall little keyboard, which, you know, there is this processor which is basically a function which will be automatically called by a server and the constant string variable or that it's passed on to this function. We'll see how it works. And I'll just be in a moment. Now, in word setup the usual stuff. We start serial communication, we start to censor, then start. We find if it is not connected, we simply print something onto the screen. Once it's connected with print, the IP address of all particular IP address a particular use the type to on to this screen of signal terminal. And then what we do here is we are creating the server over here. It's a server dot on with a get request. What we are trying to do is we are trying to serve this particular page, how and where. So the pages index and the score estimate. That's basically the piece that we are trying to serve within the scope. So the same page, it's specified over here. So what is on with index is Stamen. And plus, this is the processing function which is being. Mentioned over here. So this processor will process the index dot HTML. And so literally this target of absolutely this target. Then there are two more functions which are associated with it itself. One is of inhumanity and deprivation. So they will also be walking alongside. So whenever someone hits a request from you, all these three functions will automatically be caught by the sun. So the page will come, then the temperature will come, and then let you intuitively recall the last line.

```
// Connect to Wi-Fi
WiFi.begin(ssid, password);
while (WiFi.status() != WL_CONNECTED)
{
  delay(1000);
  Serial.println("Connecting to WiFi...");
}

// Print ESP32 Local IP Address
Serial.println(WiFi.localIP());

// Route for root / web page
server.on("/", HTTP_GET, [](AsyncWebServerRequest *request){
  request->send_P(200, "text/html", index_html, processor);
});
server.on("/temperature", HTTP_GET, [](AsyncWebServerRequest *request){
  request->send_P(200, "text/plain", readDHTTemperature().c_str());
});
server.on("/humidity", HTTP_GET, [](AsyncWebServerRequest *request){
  request->send_P(200, "text/plain", readDHTHumidity().c_str());
});

// Start server
server.begin();
}

void loop() {
```

It's sort of a random beginning. Every other operation of the server will happen in the server thread that is walking in parallel. Nothing else is added in the loop. If you want, you can add something in your to make sure it should not have any delay routines because delays interrupt. Delays stop all the interruptions. You also stop the server from work. So this is the working of the DSD sensor and it's this sort of intervention program. I will understand this initially. If you are in any of the initial stages, I would still suggest that you don't go into understanding every line of the code. You just get going with it. Slowly and steadily, everything will start making sense to you.

# WHAT IS INTERNET OF THINGS

Hi. Let's get started. By taking a total understanding of what exactly is Internet of Things and what are the fundamentals of it. Now, since this is the primary agenda of the schools, that is to understand the , it is important for us to have a clear understanding about the fundamentals of , and that's what we are going to achieve in this particular project.

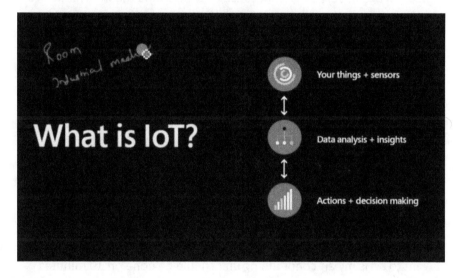

So let's get started. Now, when we say or when you say Internet of Things, what are the things that should come in our minds primarily? And if we think about it in this way, the Internet of Things, it's primarily sensing the information from a moment. Now, when I say a moment, it's a very broader context. The environment can be of a simple role. An involvement can be an industrial involvement or an industrial machinery or something. The involvement which we have to sense can be jungle or atmospheric, whether it can be an entire building. It can be a running vehicle. It can be almost anything. Wherever you can connect a sensor that becomes an environment or that particular location for your departure, it can be what? It can be your energy meter. It can be a completed building's building management system. Can do almost anything. The primary thing, it's the environment from where you are sensing the information and this information when you sensitive in a conventional context, what we do is we simply display somewhere locally using a display. But in , the purpose is basically to transfer this information to an Internet based location somewhere on the Internet where we want to store this information. And what's the purpose of storing this information on Internet? The purpose is very simple. We want to perform some kind of data analysis and insights, try to find out some insights on this information. Now, why? To send it on Internet? The reason is, again, very simple, because once you send the information to Internet, you can be anywhere in the world and you can still access the information. So I may very well have my house in one part of the world, and I may be and I can be very easily able to look at the parameters in my house from another continent. Same can apply for a vehicle which is running in Europe and I want to have a complete view of how it is going. Where is my transport going when it is being well, where it is being completely offloaded or where it can be, but it is moving in the location. I can monitor that sitting in India or something like that. So gathering information from an informant, sending it over the Internet to perform some data analysts, why we perform the dialysis so that we can make better decisions about our business, about our system, about our home. I'm going to my home right now, and it's a very hot summer day. So what I want to do is my air conditioning unit should be done on 10 minutes before I go to home so that no limits call out. Simple as that. It's a very simple consumer electronic application. On the other hand, if you want to see the analytics of a production plant sitting in your office, which is located in probably another city, then also can be helpful in gathering the intent of production information and create field reports about the production for you. The applications of are not figuratively, not just as a matter of speech, but literally limitless. There is almost no limits to what you can do with Internet of Things. So as I said, there are things from which you gather the information.

| Things | Connectivity | People & Processes |
|---|---|---|
| (Sensors, actuators, MCU/MPU, network, energy, firmware) | (PAN, LPWAN, Cellular) | (IoT Cloud, Machine Learning, AI) |

These things are sensors, actuators, some microprocessor microcontroller units, which can do the information from there, some connectivity to which it can send the information or the data to some Internet based sources. And then you process that information in a very simple format. And this is how I would like to explain on this. I would like to outline I know the most important part of this entire picture is the thing itself. That is the first point of that is the first you can see the starting point of an idea application isting. Ting means the environment from which you are reading the information. The first point of hard of that electronic part of it which senses the information and some sort of work of cloud. This usually is consisting of this primal blocks, as you can see. So there can be input sensors and variety of different forms. There can be output devices like the air conditioning unit. I'll give you an example which needs to turn on and off.

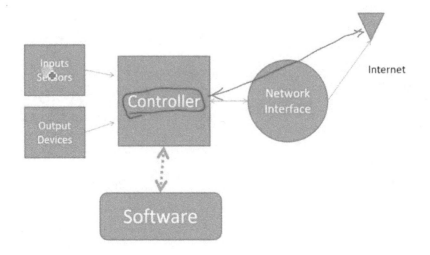

Then there is a controller which has to process this information and using the network interface, the controller will then send this information over to Internet. So this is about external communication. It will send the required information, it will assume the required information and then perform some unknown action. If there is not enough action involved, then it will simply keep reading the input values from the sensors and logging it onto the internet. So and to do all these things, this controller request a complete piece of reconfigurable software embedded into it. So this in a very general purpose format, you can see as one part or the endpoint of your thing. Now here the controller can be DSP 32. The controller can be a complete, sophisticated system like Raspberry Pi or a very basic microcontroller. It can be any such thing. The reason why we prefer ESP 32 is because it comes with onboard capability of connecting to Wi-Fi, and it is also low cost. Raspberry Pi also comes with life, but the cost is not suitable or justifiable for a single unit fours, in the sense that if you have to create so is better, to do therefore is the best and ideal candidate to perform this particular kind of system. Now, the question here is, first of all, what are the network interfaces we are talking about? Why is it the only network interface that is used? And I are definitely not. See, the point here is we want to do what I do is just have one more slide over here. So that I can give this information. So the point primarily it's. Just a minute. We want information that is coming from some sources to be sent over to cloud. Now it can take different groups to reach that position. To give you an example, in one of my project, what we did was all the sensors were connected via a Zigbee protocol. Because my if I was not available. And there were number of sensors. This is one sensitive tool. And Alexis and all this information is collected at one location. And that one location was having a computer. Through the interface. It was receiving the information and then the computer was sending the information out. My lab. Now this is one topology. In a practical situation, you can correct any number of such topologies, maybe everywhere. Why, Orlan may not be possible. In that case, the controller chips like the photon can also be used, which comes with the capability of directly connecting a SIM card, which now becomes a SIM card. Connected connectivity. What happens? You can leverage the inability of a similar internet facility and directly connect to cloud. So wi fi is one option. LAN is another option. Bluetooth is also used sometimes. Zigbee is also used and very popular. Currently Lora is also being used now by Lora is getting popular because you can send larger or you can send information over larger distances, a much less power use in Europe. So if you have a coal mine or something which is located at a remote location that is no internet connectivity like this, then you cannot see as Lora. However, this is not the point of current discussion. Currently, we are assuming that we are having ESP 32 with why. If I don't do it and we are trying to understand how we can build systems based on it, but since we are starting here, so my job to give you an overview of all the available things which are present out there.

# Applications

- Consumer
- Industrial
- Commercial
- infrastructure

Now, as stated before, the applications are literally limitless, primarily where we work or when I primarily work. Is this for various consumers industrial, commercial and infrastructure. But as I said, there are a number of different applications, which also includes variables as well. That's connected cars, connected buildings, hospitals, connected manufacturing and many things. Now, what are the requirements of a proper architecture? The most important requirement of an IP architecture. When you are creating your next project, it's whatever you design. It should be able to handle the proper hardware and software heterogeneity if possible. And I'm saying if possible, it should have a single or not more than two different programming languages.

# IoT Architecture Requiremen ts

Handle proper hardware and software heterogeneity.

Reliability

Scale

Data latency.

Be secure by design

Lower barriers to entry: evaluate -> prototype -> deploy

Manufacturable

And all the hardware should be easily talking, using the software with each of the your hardware, whatever you select, should be reliable and scalable so that even if you are creating one system or if you have lives of 10, 000 systems, it should be able to handle it. The data latency is one point which comes into the picture, but we will discuss later latency later. Some applications may require a very immediate response or a very limited data vision, but most of the applications are not hard. Real-Time Systems A little bit of small delay in data transmission is always the important thing is the architecture should be secured by design because in the end it is going to be an IP protocol and IP protocols or anything that is going on Internet is Heikkinen. So if you're design is by by the design itself, if your system is secure, then you can minimize those kind of threats. Lastly, if you are using or creating battery operated systems, the power consumption is important and if it is a microcontroller based system you are creating, it should be manufactured and built. Not every project that you create are required to be manufactured. For example, if a company comes to me asking they want do they want to implement smart manufacturing in their industry, then I don't need a manufactural solution. I need a custom built solution which is suitable for Dutch company. But tomorrow, if a customer comes to you and asks for a home, a safety monitoring system which can have a prediction, it's going to have gas leak inspection, fire detection, those kind of things. Then it has to be a manufactural system. So there are two ways to implement and I would approach. One is when you are creating project and another one is when you are creating products. I'll discuss that later on in something. So there are different technologies involved. One is examining then communications protocols which are involved. And then there are a variety of different hydrous. Why are Europeans of Korea is very lucrative. That is. It is simply because usually you will not find a single person who is good in hardware as well as communication with the girls as well as with them. Therefore, if you muster the skill, you become a very valuable asset in terms of employment as well as you become a valuable resource as a supplier of AI systems. What you want to do eventually is choice show. But my job is to explain you the benefits of becoming good. I. Now, when I say you want to send information to cloud, what do I mean by that? So by nature, you're going to have two different types of cloud service. One is, if you haven't heard about it, Louis or Google Cloud or Microsoft as well, something like that. So these are major custom designs with major cloud providers. You need to take this approach when you are creating a product. You cannot afford to use in a pure psychotic or as variety hub when you are creating a single person. When you are creating a single project. This is Colette's platform as a service when you are creating a single project. The recommended way is to use software as a service product that a number of different software as a service platforms which are maybe made IAP platforms. All you have to do is create an account over there, then start to start sending data out of there. The visualizations are really analytics obviously, and all you need to do is simply configure them and spell your requirements and spell your needs. Now, throughout the project of this particular project, we will have more focus on the suspect, because this kind of this kind of budgets are easy to create, quick to learn, and suitable for most of the project requirements, and also gives an insight about how you will create the product when the time comes for each. So these are the primarily two different choices of cloud service bus allsorts. Not much option in bus. Yes, of project there are, but they're not limited to 5 to 10 different options. So and you will eventually end up in something that is standard like Amazon on IBM or Microsoft will cloud. But when it comes to choosing a softer, just sort of the spectrum, then there is a ton of choice. Literally, there will be 50 plus different options available. I'm just giving you some names simply as a reference. So the thing works, is there everything? Is there sense of cloud device, cloud things? Big numeric out of all these things can speak, is a very, very powerful platform and it is also available for you to evaluate and not only to evaluate. Three You can also do a project on things speak which can be in production for quite some time or quite long.

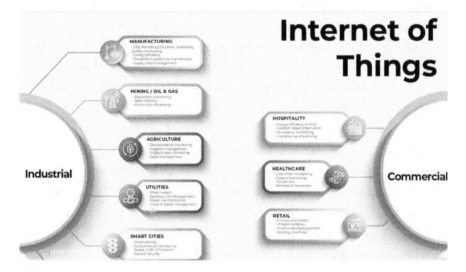

So this is a very what are you going to see or what have you off? How are you this distance? What are the different cloud options available? What are the IRP projects? What are the products? I just kind of hinge when you would use suspect form and then use cross-platform. Now, after this project, what will study in our next project is will try to understand what are the different protocols used in . And then we're trying to create a simple application using BSD to do an ESB to do.

# PROTOCOLS AND THINGSPEAK

Hi. In this project, we'll try to see some protocols which are used in creation, fire resistance. And we'll also try to see one of the platforms which we will be using to create based product or activist project. In our project. There are actually like many different protocols involved in creation of a single system. But for the simplicity, what we are doing here is we are assuming that we have a network connected device like SBT to address the device with on a computer routers, for example. And we already have an IP connectivity through Wi-Fi. And now the protocol that we're going to discuss about this communication from use Win32 to Cloud. What are the different protocols which are used? And I'm also going to give you most popularly used political names over here. I'm not covering the of communication in the context of disproject. So here we are talking about Wi-Fi connectivity between Yosemite to the cloud. So there are three very popular use protocols which are employee maturity. And it should be in terms more advanced message protocol, amputating arms, sort of message skewing element to support. And you know about the hypertext transfer protocol on hypertext transfer protocol secure that it should be as they should it be is usually be tied sent and received to get and post request. And this by far is the simplest of all the communication protocols. However, it should be has its own drawbacks. The package size or the size of the message to send and receive the response is a bit higher than what is written. And you didn't. And therefore it shouldn't be. And also this seems to be the slowest among all of them. Then group is a very specialist protocol used when the latency on very low latency is large, but the most general purpose protocol are the most commonly used. Protocol in almost follow this instance are the winner of a protocols its end duty. So what we are going to do now is we're going to see how we can send data to issue TB. We will also try to see a platform that supports it should be data transfer, and then we are going to give a little treatment to what is included. And then we will try to understand a platform. I'll try to create a project with the platform which supports intuitive protocol and send the information to him to do it. So we are going to see how we can send information from your strategy to using it as well as using muted.

### **Project 1** : Temperature and Humidity Logging in Cloud

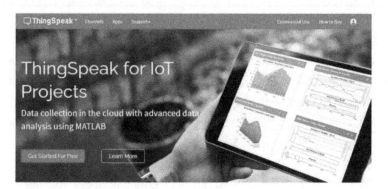

So I have shown you some of the cloud platform names previously and out of that this one is one of the most interesting ones, which is called it's pink speak, not called now textbook supports but imputed as the next step. But in the free account it only supports issue and that is enough for us to do a lot of different experimentation which we are going to see now.

# Thingspeak

- Free for up to 8 fields
- 15 second refresh time
- Lots of online apps can be developed for analytics

So it is it takes three primarily gives you three data storage for interviews, maximum eight different information like let's say if you are creating a system or if you are creating a project for home automation or industrial automation, then it means that you can send it since that information's to vehicles. You can send information every 15 seconds faster than that is not allowed in the free account. And there are lots of different online apps which can be developed for analytics with things. So I guess enough of the box and let's try to understand what is in speak. So let me open a browser and let me look at the platform to speak. Now, as I was saying, you think speak is suitable for projects. If you open the page you will also see the same thing. Speak for IT budgets. It doesn't say things speak for products. It's variety projects. Now what is the difference? You will understand that when we create one system. First of all, let's see how you can start using things. So all you need to do is first go to the sign in options, and then if you don't have an account, then simply click on the create one project and have to put your email, address, your location, first name and last. Lastly, after that, it will send you an email for verification. After clicking that email, you will be able to create a password onto speak. It's very simple and straightforward. So what I'm going to do is I'm simply going to log in to my account over here. So I have an account on the script, which I will be using. And my boss, which. And simply click on sign in.

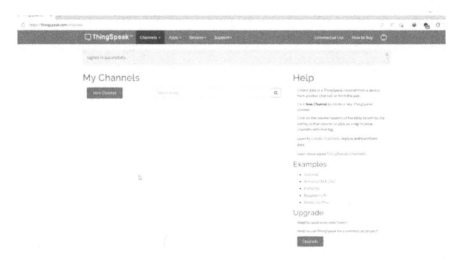

So when you create a new account on spec, this is how something will look like. Definitely you will be going through all these examples and everything, but that is something we can-do later. For now, let's just try to understand the basics of the fundamentals of things. You will see channels over here. You will see apps, devices and support. And these are some of the steps. Now, when you create your first account on things to begin with, you want to create your first projects one of the subsidy to date. So the very first thing you need to do is take a new channel. Give it some me. So let's say projects one then we then I just started down here temperature and humidity and cremation of mantle. The name and description is completely optional. Whatever you want suitable you can put your Q as mentioned before. Thanks. Which allows up to eight seats in a free account in a single channel. So for now it isn't able to be for films. Let's call the first. Well that's then. Well. It is also optional. You can call it whatever you want them to. Then let's say humidity and humidity. Whatever you want, you can call it. Eventually, you will not be accessing this space by their name over here, but you will simply access them by three. One, three, two, four, three, three, four. Like that. No other changes are basically required. But you can, however, navigate as you may find. Which. Once this is done, it will save this channel. And as soon as you save the channel, you will see that your IAP dashboard has them created for you. Now this organized mode is coming up with, if you'll see, four different graphs of four different charts, so a available data monitoring system is ready for. All you need to do is start pushing information over here and you will see the data points right coming with you next time to see something. By sending information. Now, there are a lot, many other things. Also, if you see our visualization, then our widgets, we are going to see all of that later. For now, I will go to the API kids because first job that I want to do is I just want to see. I just want to send some value and see how it looks. And then we will see how we can do the same thing using SB 30. So see a light, a channel food if you go to a snack is you will find that ah, Hewlett-Packard's one is two right and one is still read and then there are sample API requests. So this is one for writing, this is one for reading and so on. What I'll do is I'll just copy this, right, channel food model and we'll try to evaluate this. Okay. I have copied it right click copy. And I will go to private. Now look me up on a notepad and just take a look at this link, what it's like. So if you see a step stupid, a production spec dot com question mark, then api underscore p is equal to some keywords and it done over here. Now let's look at the key again. This is the same API key that you have the right API over here. So you can use this one and simply replace the scheme with your account settings. And you can send some information and how the information is written. Look at this sample here and see the one is it. Let's say my first value. It's 11. 5 degrees Celsius, my friend, when it's temperature. Let me put this directly. If I look up in this URL. And all you need to do is simply open a browser. Enter that all. I will go to private view again. You can see there is no data point over here. And I will simply hit enters. Now you will see the responses. One. This foster quest has been sent. And now let's look at this shot in the sea. My first data point has been to distinct along with the date and time and as it. Now if you want to can send information on two things. Speak by simply moving like this and feel one. Can we add another one? Of project. Let's put it like this. And then two is equal to 25. 3 if we modify the first one from 11. 5 to 11. 9. Let us add more face. And the three is equal to 74% and then the four is equal to 43%. Let's see all of it. Remember that this data will only be updated every so often. So let's hit this one. You get a response to just wait. You can see all four data points here. Now simply make some changes over here again. 11 points to 25. 8 instead of 74. Let's make it 77 for serious looking for deflate again hit enter. Third request is gone and now you will see the data points again getting updated. Getting it. Now, if you keep using this request every now and then by making some changes, your first project is done. I know, I know you have not sent in ideal information, but just imagine if you can send your vehicle temperature information and with it information, then your data will start coming right over here.

This is the bare bones project without sensors, without any hardware, which you can experiment to it. Now, of project, we will try to send this information through ISP 32 and we will try whatever is available in things speak to make our projects more just. That's it for this project, guys. I hope you will be able to experiment with this thing. And from the next project we will try to send this information from your scooter due to you reading from sensors or what am I planning to live on? Do our thing, speak the couch.

# SENDING VALUES TO THINGSPEAK FROM ESP32

Hi. In the last project, we have seen the basics of things. We have seen the account creation on things. We are going to be held accountable to attract the cent. Some dummy panels, write a lot of things, pick a bunch, and this project will try to create up to them with sense the temperature and humidity information that we are getting from the HD one one or two to do sensor on button speak. Now in order to complete this program, you don't need any particular lab. All you need is the on one level of the issue to connect body and that's all. So this is the only library that you're going to need the boosters and stuff like that by now. Let's look at the code. Now, what I'll do is I'll also show you something which you should not be using. Okay. So let me show you. So there is also an official speak library which is provided for our DINO and I have distributed guides. Believe me, it's not worth it. So it will work sometimes, then sometimes it will be broken. And if you're trying to use a program which shows this particular library, I would say, please avoidthat program. The best way is to directly use the model for posting the town booking suite. And that works without any favor. So just be sure that you don't get indulged into the celebrity Alderson Official Library. I'm telling you to stay on the assignment. Now, this is my. This is my dashboard. So if you know that I had created four different fields. But currently, I'm going to send only two values over here. So one will be temperature and another will be humidity.

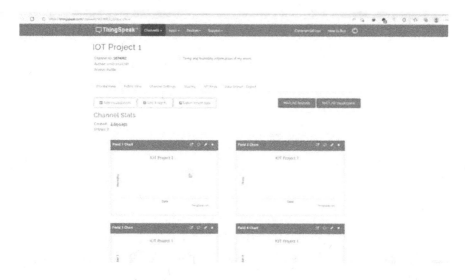

Now, let's look at the cool. We'll walk through the quarter completely. So this is the program that we're going to use. Now, if you look at the first two, three libraries, so this one is still active. I think if I going to find out about this one, it's to include the utility client library, which is helpful for us to post, which should be request. And this is the most elaborate. This is the DHT connection bin, which you know about, and this is the type of dish dispenser that we are using. Lastly, we create an instance of this level three quality HD so that we can use it. Then you will see we have the A society or the I. D. and password over here. And this right over here is your thing. Speak. You want it. This is the entire one which we hitting before also. If you remember, the only thing that you need to add here, here, right over here is please replace it with your right API key. So you need to replace this last part with the key that you see in your account. Where do we see that? In API keys. Over here. So this one is mine. That's why I'm showing you this one.

```
const char* ssid = "Robotics Lab";   // your network ssid (name)
const char* password = "Robotics@321";   // your network password

// your thingspeak channel url with api_key query
String serverName = "https://api.thingspeak.com/update?api_key=XXXXXXXXXXXXXXXX"; // please replace it with your write API Key

void setup()
{
   Serial.begin(9600); // Opens up the serial port with a baudrate of 9600 bits per second

   WiFi.begin(ssid, password); // Attempt to connect to wifi with our password
   Serial.println("Connecting"); // Print our status to the serial monitor
   // Wait for wifi to connect
   while(WiFi.status() != WL_CONNECTED)
   {
      delay(500);
      Serial.print(".");
   }
   Serial.println("");
   Serial.print("Connected to WiFi network with IP Address: ");
   Serial.println(WiFi.localIP());
   delay(2000);
   dht.begin();
}

void loop()
{
   if(WiFi.status()!== WL_CONNECTED)
```

Apart from that, let remove anything unnecessary that I had. Right now I'm just going see, they'll begin so that I can put in some debugging messages over here. Then we are doing if I begin, this is the passage and then we'll print something that we are trying to correct as soon as and now the program or this part. It's basically as long as we not connected to why fine. Or what we do is my photo status will simply try to do my status. And if it is not connected, then we wait for 500 millisecond and some people in the dark on them. So that just gives a feeling that the product, as long as or the moment it gives connected, will get this message connected to. I find it to work with the IP address and what I do is I will also add a deliverable. So it will connect to your local pipeline network and then it will print the idea which has been assigned to the ISP today. Then what we do is we do the BSD dot begin function called which will initialize our use to 2%, which has been connected. Now I told you that free account of things will only allow you to send data every 15 seconds. So for every 15 seconds of data sending, what you need to do is you need to be it up 15 seconds after every iteration. So in my look, what I have done is if the line five status is connected, then we are going to proceed. How we proceed in what we post is mentioned over here. So it should be client? It should be. This is an instance of a library that we are creating. Then with the humidity and temperature, hence we bring them on to the terminal just to get an information about it. And now we create a you what of this is the scene you are told that you are going to create, which should be in the browser. So this data server name right over here then. And if anyone is able to add your first variable and includes golden and second variable, if you have and the tree and food four, simply go on and engage the same question. And then what we do is we don't bring in you are a lot C SGA. So the C is still basically passes the pointer to the string to this function. And now this will be you. And what will do it will try to get after this function. So here the big image. And here we try to hit the request after the request. Is it? We're trying to read that response into a sticky response. And this response score must be 200. So anything greater than zero, if the response scored is greater than zero, means we have some issue request, then we print. That is typically response code. If it is not greater than zero, then what we have to look into to look you. Then it should be the end and a delay of 15, 000 millisecond or 15 seconds. So this will happen if it's connected. Otherwise you will get the message.

I disconnected after every moment for a disconnected message. Let's look at the emails deposited milliseconds so that there is a difference. Otherwise, if the Viper gets disconnected in between, you will be hit with three or four messages. Now I have started uploading the code. It will take some time. Meanwhile, let's go to channel settings. And do you have the channel so that there is not a single data point on our channel? In our view. So this is my channel. This is the idea. Now the program is being compiled and then it will be uploaded to the to board. Now, this is the simplest and the most practical way to use things like that. So I would recommend using this way only. Once the program is uploaded with just open the city to monitor. Trying to see the outcome. Code is downloaded. Connected to our site with IP address. It's with temperature within humidity and the response score is to drench political support admins success. Now let's open this board over here and see if we can get the data point. So we have. Okay. The first one which we have sent this temperature on the second one, which we have seen humidity that'sof stick and creating the channel. Let's call the first one adds temperature and the second one ends with it. After 15 seconds, you start getting another data point as well. So I don't think 15 seconds have elapsed. So after 15 seconds, you will again see this message and that is this, humanity is this. And then this line and another response which. Let's see. And I given 15 I have given one additional. So that is 1 to 2 seconds. Let's remove that one and we applaud. Meanwhile, this is your things, big dashboard or what I can say is this is the first IAP project. So by default the name of your channel will come here. I project when I deposit and here is the temperature. You can also modify whatever you want to show over here. So the title is Let's roll them then I want to show. This is my room humidity. I did some tea, but I want to show. Let me see the quote. It's uploaded. It's going on. And supporters applauded. Now it is connected because the other data point, the data point it sends is also this 200 differentdata point right over here. There.

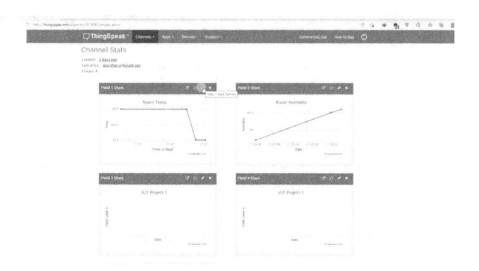

You can see we have got the two points. This one is temperature and humidity by default. The charts over here will be automatically adjusted of dynamically adjusted. Just go here and play around with the settings, whatever you want to happen over here. So you can change time scale. You can change your average median. What do you want to display on X? What you want to display on y. So y for example, for us in Spain exits M in BGC. So in that way. So why it's. Value products and exits include. So this way you'll start getting the points. Now I am not even going into my Arduino, Paul, but as you can see, the temperature logging had started. Now, this is the Batman PIN Stick project that you will be doing. Apart from that. Of project, there are other things that can also be done, like you can add against weight. You can download the data into your computer and like many other things, we'll see that in the next project. So that's it for this project, guys. What I'll do is I'll keep the same core running in my institute you do. And then we'll experiment further on this part over here. Till then, what I'm going to do is I'm going to keep this alive. It is coming so that I want to monitor the data for some time. Let's see. That's still out next week. Thank you, guys.

# DATA VISUALIZATIONS IN THINGSPEAK

Now that we have seen a sample data uploading from things speak on from the as we told you to go things we cloud let's see what other things we can do in seed or apart from just viewing individual assertions. However, let's give this one thing in your mind. Whatever my experiences out of the kind of projects that I have gone to monitoring is perhaps the most important application people use a UTI for. There is a cloud control facility available, of project, but usually in industrial sense it does not use. So things speak of something which would turn out to be very good for you if you are creating an industrial project. Now this is my dashboard, so I am not having the other at the end, so let me just delete them. So this is how I'm getting my data right over here. First of all, let's see what, apart from these two views we can have. So we can see there is an active visualizations button right over here and it should click that. You can see there are a number of different things which can be shown, as I told you. Now, if you don't go there and if you just go here on this tab, so there are visualizations and then there are widgets. There are some widgets which are built inside itself. For example, if I see a numeric display. And connected to frequent and let's call it room temperature. Then you will also be able to see a room temperature widget coming right over here. So it has been doing some rounding off. But let's take the decimal point temperature. And now it will show you an exact room temperature. In case. If you don't want this, you can also have a gauge. Previously we had to write down a good gauge code, but now it has got integrated in the thin speaker itself. So you can show the main value, you can show the max value of let's see if it is room temperature showed that the max value will never be more than 50, 55 or 60.

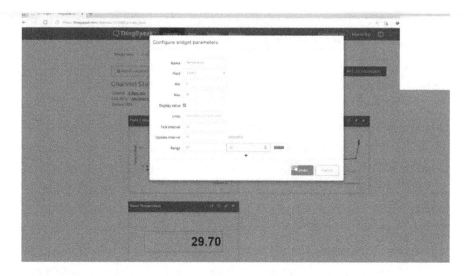

29.70

You can also show something like that from range 35 and onwards of 35 to 68, which means it's 14, something like that. And then let's choose the unit as degrees Celsius and create a gauge. Now I'll just delete this one. So here we have a gauge against for temperature. And similarly, I can also have a gauge for humidity.

So humidity is going to the genetics percentage. Lip sitch. Can you see that? This way you can customize your visualization in a bit more fashionable ways so that you get to see some different visualization, some different look at the visualization. And if you want to go beyond that, if you really want to go beyond that, you can also go to apps and then you can go to visualizations and create your own visualization. I don't want to go into that immediately now because I'm considering this to be a beginning of a new project. And for most of the industrial applications, if you have noticed how many visualizations is usually everything that is required and about from having visualizations. Another thing we want is to be able to export the data. Now you see you have this filled one fill to fill people for the time that you can export. Let me export the temperature data at CAC over here. And let's see how it looks like. Can you do some analytics about it? Can you do some operations about it? You definitely can do about it and just see. So this is the I. D. and this is a free one. You could all the pilots stored over here. Into this excel or see us. We find based upon that we can become more analytics, create more charts and visualizations in Excel or in any other way as you want. These are just some of the visualization additions that you can do the things. And next project will try to see how you can create some analytics over this visualization.

# ANALYTICS IN THINGSPEAK

Now we have the things visualizations created. You have seen the images as well as numeric display. Now let's come to some sort of analytics if we can do that. And the most important analytics, whenever you are dealing with any such kind of industrial project, we may be sending out email alerts. So whenever some particular panel went on some particular value list that exceeds a particular point, then you may want to just run to analytics. Now, how do you do that? That's what you're going to see in this project. So let's begin.

Now in order to create analytics inside things, you may go to apps and you can see that a number of different apps which are available, out of which what I'm going to see for now is react. But first, let's go one by one. So first of all, there is a MATLAB analysis, MATLAB analysis. It's something which is a MATLAB code can be run for whatever you are going to do. So I have something over here and show you how to use that. Then there is matlab visualizations, so I don't use this one. I'll just village this one. So you can write down MATLAB code and create visualizations in macro. Then you can go to plugins and here you can see there is a custom plugin that you can create that is charged with multiple series and you can create a Google image. If you go to custom, then you can literally get any kind of extreme in code that can do this from your filters and display anything the way you want. Then they just take it. Here you can rip based upon whatever films that are coming over here. Then there is time control. Time control means you can create something. You can do something timely. For example, if you have production that is being monitored, then they can do a time control. At the time of shift ending, you can shoot animal. Then there is React, which you are going to see done back and think back and think is the DP again, some additional controls with which you can send information back to the hospital to board now. And lastly, the distinguished studio. So I am not using either of them. Let me just go through it and delete all. Now what I want to do is I want to shoot an email whenever a temperature of value or something goes beyond a particular point. So when you want to shoot email or if you want to do some things, analytics, what do you need to do is four things quick analytics processes. That is simple. First thing is you need to have a MATLAB analytics code. I'm going to give you that code inside this presentation only so that you can simply copy and paste it like this red elementary school will be used as a reaction for something. How? Let's see them. First of all, let me put it all over here. Now let me go to apps and first go to MATLAB analysis. Here I have this code written already. I'm just going to put it over here. How to have that, how to do that every day. I will show you what I do with you. So just put it as a text. I have put it here. You can use it directly. Now in order to use this MATLAB analysis score, what you need is an alert API. So the very first thing that you will have to do is let's go first of all to channel. My channel, for example. Here, you will see a number of different things. So it is public view. The rationale springs that it's sharing that it's API key data, data input output settings, all these different settings.

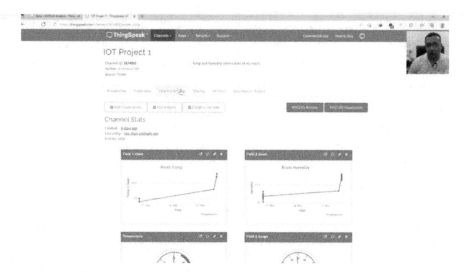

Now what we want to do is we want to have a particular alert. Now on the surface over here, you will not see the alert API. So just go to your name and your profile. When you go to your profile, even see an alert. API alerts api.

This alert is API will always start with the peak and some metrics followed by it. What you need to do is you need to copy this alert API key from here. And if I open the code, then you have to insert it right over here. So this is. Ah, this should be your alert API key. Keep this project in mind. We have to replace the alert API. Okay. So you have to replace this alert with you. Now, since you can see I have already copied this one. Put it in my MATLAB code over here. I don't want to repeat that. Let's go back to MATLAB analysis. And what you do here is you simply click on New. Then you just pick custom most architecture. And just based that entire pool with you. No need to do any other thing. Simply piece to go here and click on see. So what do you do? It's you go. First step is you go to your profile, then you copy the alerts API. Okay, this one. Then you go to apps and matlab analysis. Then you create. So I created it. And let me just do one thing if we do it from beginning. Just let me delete everything that I have created so that it becomes easier for us to understand. So we will do MATLAB analysis. Then your account will not have anything to do with you. So my channel, this is your default view, which shows you all the variables and parameters. You go to apps, MATLAB analysis. You create new. You just use a custom template. And then you have to be still go to live here. That's all you have just listed as objects. That's nothing else is required to be done. This is a large body. Maybe if you are creating an alert for temperature exceeding. So let's call it temperature. Obsidian from Sequoia. Whatever is, there's point. This is a subject body. Let's change the subject. Whatever you want. This message from you can speak cloud. That's all. Okay. And now let's click on Severe. Let's call it my MATLAB email code so that you can easily identify this. Now, once you created your analysis, the next thing you do is you go to the act. Okay, so live with some resistance. So first go to profile copy, alert API key, then go to MATLAB analysis score, then go to app's MATLA Banalysis. Neil then face the board and then see. Now go to apps again and then the package. Now here, when you do new the act, then it'll ask what exactly you want to do. So let's say the act one instead of the action, let me call it in. Sending them. All right. Something like that. Condition tribalistic. Numeric best frequency on data insertion. You can also do it like every 10 minutes. Anything. Do 10 minutes should be good. Because on data insertion, if you do, then it will start sending the requests multiple times. So for now we are doing testing. So let's do on data insertion. Now condition is if Channel one are in this channel project, then three one temperature is greater then. Now let's see. What is my current temperature going on? I guess it should be 30 something. It is 29 point something. So if it is greater than 31, for example. Then you have to select an action. So this is your react condition and what should be your action? There are three options targets DPI, MATLAB, analysis, anything which can quit something if you want. Let's shows MATLAB analysis over here and then you have to select the four that you have previously. That is my matlab import. Now run action. Only the first time the condition is met. We can choose this. We can choose this. An action each time the condition is which for us. Let's use this one because we are running in free account. And if I keep sending the requests multiple times, then I may be barred from usage. So let's give it a run action. Only the first time condition is match. Now let me open my Gmail account. With which the speaker speakerphone descriptor. And we'll just wait here till we get a new message. So let's see if this reacts. Now that he acted saved. No. The channel is over here. Now, all we need to do is we need to increase the temperature. Okay. We have said more than 31. We also get to see what is our temperature going on over here. So disjointed and current. Now all I'm going to do is I'm going to blow some hot air into it.

I'll just put the camera right over my heart of it. So that you get to have a look over which of. Okay. That's the sensor. Now. I have learned some it but the object sequences 15 seconds so we are not we didn't get more than 15seconds faster. It will increase the humidity at the same time. It is also expected to increase the temperature a little. So it's 30. We reached up to 30, but I want something more, so I'll just close my room as well and let's do a bit more experimentation with. Sorry. Okay. So let's acknowledge. Is greater than 30. I guess my condition was greater than 31. Now I have blown enough air into it. I guess we should get the party greater than three point. Meanwhile, we just went through the app. Check the condition. What it is greater than 30. So let's do some more. And okay, we've got 31. 2 and you'll see, we got two things that. And you see the email instantly. So temperature extended from set point. We also get to see the time and ability. Well, the efforts finally paid off. And, yeah, we should have done it to humiliate him, because you would do deals with U. S. interests, but nevertheless. So this way you can create your visualization as well as analytics with things. There is lot more to study and love to experiment with here, and I will leave it to you to continue experimentation with things. The same, believe me, with the same feature set with the same three conferences. Of project we should not use it for commercial use, and you should purchase it for when you want to use it for commercial purposes. But when you have a client and your client wants you to give a demonstration, you simply can't be just for the demonstration purposes because they don't know whether it will work or whether it will not work. And therefore, in such cases, having a pink slick visualization like this or having things analytics like this, even in a free account, helps a lot. So go on and experiment with this kind of visualizations. Most importantly, if you go for and see, you also can get a ten speed app. So there is a little app called View placed on. I don't know if that's visible to you, but this is the name of the app. So Think View is the name of the app. And if you open thing you. Then you can simply add your channel lady over here and you can see the visualizations even in mobile. So now for that said, what you can do is you can make your channel public, which I already have done. I just have to put my channel over here. So it is one six. Seven four. 092. 1674092 that sort of have originated over here. And then and simply search footage. And you can see you'll get the visualizations of. On your smartphone, you can easily give a demonstration like this to a customer before you have to install a system. That's simple as that. I sincerely, really do hope that it helps with this kind of experimentation. So just keep going on with that experimentation and see what more you can do. It can speak.

# ADAFRUIT PROJECT - PART 1

Hi. Now that we have seen some basic idea, we have got some basic idea about what is the protocol. Let's try to implement them using a real life situation, writ of different laws of this gold in the fruit. Previously we have experimented with things speak and you can also experiment using intuitive things speak. But I just thought of adding a new cloud service to make things a bit more interesting.

Adafruit IO

We now endeavor IO is a managed service which is provided by dot com in New York and it's again three, 4 to 5 different foods you can enter in bridge. Let's try to see what is it? I'll help you use it. And how to experiment with it. Using your suite to do to. Now, this particular service is very peculiar and very interesting. You can create very nice looking and very visually stunning visualizations of right over here. And to do that, we will be using. But again, just to summarize some fundamentals over here for you. So let me tell you. In any case, when you have to use amputee, you needed the amputated bow. Then you need your particular user name and password. And then you need to have your topic amputee to topic. So your amputee topic name must be mentioned. You publish to this topic, you subscribe to this topic. You can publish as a let's subscribe. A single device can be publisher, subscriber or book. So these are some of the fundamentals. And the code that I'm going to show you now here is not only limited to you, but it is also genericand juridical so that you can utilize it in any other situations as well. Now let's see what we need to do with that type. So we need to go to in order for you to create a free account over here. And then we'll try to understand the different things which are present into it. So this one is IO . 4. com. Let me just log out, because as long as I've signed in, I will not see the team yet. So this is ironed you right after dark on the Internet of Things. And it is literally the easiest way to create applications. You can use it for personal experimentation as well as you can also use it for any professional purpose. If you're using it for personal experimentation, you have three accounts with 30 data points, which means you can send data once every 2 minutes and then sorry, once every 2 seconds, and then you have30 days of free storage and you can create some actions as well. You have to go to Stanford to get it over here. And I'll explain that to you again, because. All you need to do is simply go and create your account over here. So get started from three, which will just ask you for first name, last name, username and password. In order to hear this, I will simply try to sign into my account, which I already have on the fridge, and I have deleted everything that I do with your right. So I want to spend your time in deleting the existing data. So when you go to your account the first time, when you create your particular account, you won't see anything over the site because it's a fresh approach. What we want to do here is we want to create a dashboard. You want to create a complete project. Now, this project that I want to create here is very simple.

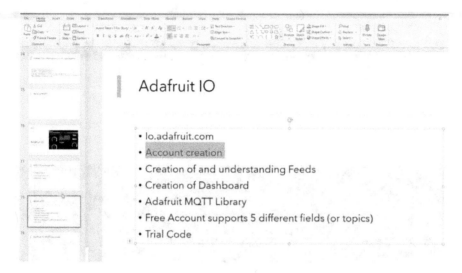

## Adafruit IO

- Io.adafruit.com
- Account creation
- Creation of and understanding Feeds
- Creation of Dashboard
- Adafruit MQTT Library
- Free Account supports 5 different fields (or topics)
- Trial Code

I want to have temperature. I want to have humidity. And I want to have a TV. I want to have this track. I want to monitor the temperature and humidity on cloud. And I also want to control it from cloud. So I'll have my relay connected to EESP 32, and I want it controlled from cloud. And also mentioning a circuit diagram, which I'm going to refer for this particular supplemental here, but this will come later. What's the most important thing is what exactly do you need? You need a temperature, you need a humidity, and you need a really. So basically speaking, you need three different things in terms of things. We call it fields. So the fields in terms of duty or in terms of particularly bucolic fields. So the very first thing you do when you create your account on your data for is graphics and you create your fields. Okay, so forgive me, I have some proofs already done, so I have deleted them. Okay. So first thing you do is you go to fields.

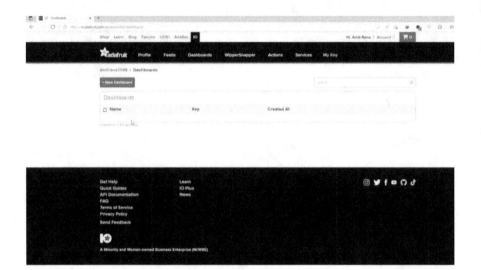

And there are no foods available. So simply go on and create a new food. Let's call the food as temperature. You can give a description if you want at the events, just skip it. So I have created a field called temperature. Then take a new field. Call it. Let's see the humidity. Save it. And since we want to control it, really, let's stick another one and let's call it really. Now this free account will support them soon to be created. Ten different feeds to be created. For now, we have created three different fields over here. Now what I do is I will simply go to dashboards. You don't have a dashboard created here. Okay. So let's create a new dashboard. Let me call it the 32 IAP project. You can give a description if you want. But now my dashboard has been created. Now just go to the dashboard and you will see literally a blank slate and this thing will be open in front of. Simply go to settings and create a new block for which you. Let me create a gauge over here. So if you go to this creative block, you can see there are a number of different visualization blocks, he continues. There is a language also there is a battery gauge dividing line that links multi-line text number, pad indicator, color pad icon, a line chart. We lost many things of this you for this experiment we just take a gauge.

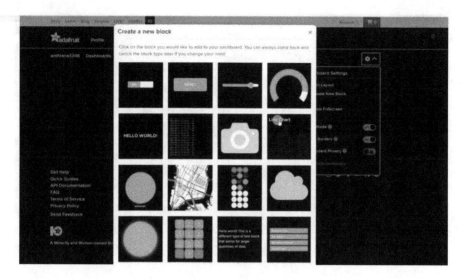

When you create a gauge, then it will ask you really want to connect. I want to connect gauge to next set temperature. So just click temperature and next to it. Now let's give a title. The title is Room Temperature, meaning value is zero. Maxwell may be 60. You can choose which red to be thinner or pick up where you want. Let's call the value to be the agency. You can also create a low and high warning value. So up to 0 to 20 is next to low and from. 435 in on words, let's say hi. Okay. So from the fire bombing that. So if your temperature, for example, it's ten, then it will show. Well, I mean, look, if it it's 21, it will show green, if you can see here. So between 21 to 34, it will be green if you make it, 35 will be. Sean again, green. If it is, let's say 36 and play on that. Ideally, you don't have to do that.

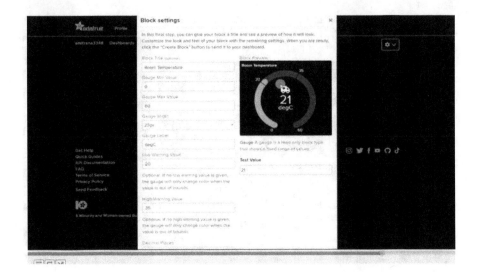

It's completely your choice. You can also select an icon over here if you want to do so. There are some icons available here. Ambulance, for example. So to ensure like that. So I don't want to issue ambulance. I want to show. Some room temperature or some kind of monitor, but. Now what we have to do is you have to select something based upon which. I don't know if we have temperature over here of March. Dee deedeedeedee. Tell them we have a thermometer. So let's create this block. We have it here. Let's create another block. This time I'll choose a gauge. I'm connected to humidity, food. I'll simply call humidity. I don't want to do anything over here. I'll simply call it as a percentage because I'm assuming humidity and percentage. And then let's create another block. This time I will take a toggle button. I will connect it to. Really? And let me call it lamb. Okay. So just clear this block. Okay. Now you can also edit the layout and just modify them to your liking. So I just put one here and another one here and this one over here. And simply, simply, if you want, you can definitely again, go to edit layout. You can also increase the size of this block so that it should look good, but it is too different now. So let me just increase this to also a little bit. So everything is eventually your choice. It's not mandated to do anything with you. Say Williams again. Let me do something. Create a new blog. And this time I'll choose a line chart connected to temperature. Again, I don't want anything else over here. Just a total temperature of what we call it, as is a stream. We have it over here. I think that should do it. So this is how you create your particular dashboard. Now, the next thing, it's connecting or giving data to this dashboard. We'll see that in our next project.

# ADAFRUIT PROJECT - PART 2

Now that we have created an entire dashboard for our usage, now it's time to send some values to this dashboard using honor code. Now what? I'm going to do it before you do that. Before you do send those values to here, let me just go to profile ones, because you're going to need or instead of going profile, you have to go to this project over here, which is called Mickey. Now when you go to myki, it will show you your username. Mine is on me. Try not to do it. And then the reason you keep this key is basically your authentication to the amputee broken off. That's what you have to use this.

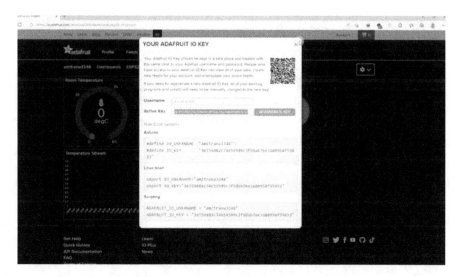

You have to copy and paste it in your code. Now I will switch to code, will try to understand the code first and then we'll try to see the. Now, this is the code over here which we use for our purpose. First thing I will do is I will walk you through the inside and before I walk you through the entire. Then we also show you the required circuit that you need to hit on this particular expert. Look at it. So we have everything. Just like before DST. It's connected to GPO 27 and this really is connected to the number.

# Circuit Wiring : DHT22 and Relay

So through this 27 number which read the temperature and humidity values and to this number 12, we will be able to control the release if needed. You can definitely go out for adding more sensors and more release as we watch. Now this particular quarter will require a utility. You most probably will already have that included celebrity as a part of our diet. If you don't have that, simply go to include library managed libraries and here you will have to search for ADA through Underscore and Q-Tip. This are a level that is given very enough, but they are not restricted to be used to it in a food server and you can use them for other purposes. The fruit and beauty. And you just have to install it. I have 1. 3. 0 installed. If you face any discrepancies, then try to use 1. 03. 0 and let me know how it works for you.

```
// some editor header

//ESP32MQTTDHT22

#include <WiFi.h>
#include "Adafruit_MQTT.h"
#include "Adafruit_MQTT_Client.h"

/************************* WiFi Access Point *********************************/

#define WLAN_SSID       "Robotics Lab"   // replace it with your Wifi Name
#define WLAN_PASS       "Robotics@321"   // Replace it with your wifi password

/************************* Adafruit.io Setup *********************************/

#define AIO_SERVER      "io.adafruit.com"
#define AIO_SERVERPORT  1883                  // use 8883 for SSL
#define AIO_USERNAME    "your_username"  // Change this to your username
#define AIO_KEY         "aio_key"        // Change this to your key

#include "DHT.h"

#define DHTPIN 27 // dht connection

#define DHTTYPE DHT22   // DHT 22  connected to pin 27

DHT dht(DHTPIN, DHTTYPE);
int rel = 12;

/************ Global State (you don't need to change this!) ******************/

// Create an ESP8266 WiFiClient class to connect to the MQTT server.
WiFiClient client;
// or... use WiFiClientSecure for SSL
//WiFiClientSecure client;
```

Now the first two lines are basically my flying fuel into the ditch and in good the decline dotage with all the good lines. Then this is the wife credentials. These are big enough for all your credentials. So you will not change the name of service. You will not change the board of server. You will definitely change the username and the e-mail. This key should be the one which I just showed you over to you. So this activity must be copied. And listening to your call like the look you. Once you do that, the inevitable later things are over. Next is you see the regular one. You draw the standard edge. Then the DHT bin is 27. The sensor type is 22 and recreate the instance of DST sensing. Lastly, we have an ADL which is to connect. And I'll just remove some comments to not make it difficult for you. Here, you create a modified plan and then you create an absolute amputated land to this land. What you have to do is you have to pass on your plan. This is like the sort of across the board number username and so that's passage. So all those values are already mentioned here we are just passing it right with you and also passing it like, okay. And then what we do here is we set up of this over here. So my first route is temperature, second visibility, third is remember the name temperature here is actually not important. This is important. The address of your feet. Now, how do you know it is forward slash grooves, forward slash temperature. Let me just go through my feet. Enough, you. Just hover over this thing and just notice this corner over here. So humidity when you see down the bottom left corner of the screen. Let's see. It should be, as I noted, as a dot com slash slash schools slash humidity. You can have as many food such as you want. You may have multiple layers, which I don't currently address of this food. If you'll see here, it's slash roots, slash humidity. Then what is my lamb? Slash foods slash really day and room temperature for slash foods for slash temperature just to mention them as forward slash routes temperature or slash severity for slash foods. So if you have more of them, simply create more such instances. Okay. Now let's go to the court. So the urgency, the terminal beginning. Then we created a relay output when initialized as our footprint made it low. Then what we do here is we again do the same thing we had done before. The one photon beginning was the Sabian password here. We wait here till we connect to I-5. Once you connect to I-5, we simply show them. Or we simply print the Fentress over here. Once that is done, what we do is we subscribe to a particular topic. I hope the concept is clear to you. So here we want to subscribe to the topic really and we want to publish to the topic temperature. I mean, so here we have subscribed to the topics and then we do the student figured. This is an important. Now this amputee connect is a function which you have to keep calling your void min also low protein so that whenever the loop executes it will check its impurity. Connection is alive. Not if it is not alive then you will have to reconnect. So therefore this is composite. It must be there on the. Now here we have created a subscription. This function is very interesting. So you create the subscription and you just wait here until sometime elapses and then you check if you have received some data or not. Now, mind, well, mind. It's currently only for really just checking one subscription. If you have more subscriptions, you'll simply copy, paste this and that if look again. So I'm checking if the subscription had some message. Yes, we do have. Then we print on the serial terminal what we have. So we may not last through.

```
// Ensure the connection to the MQTT server is alive (this will make the first
// connection and automatically reconnect when disconnected).  See the MQTT_connect
// function definition further below.
MQTT_connect();

// this is our 'wait for incoming subscription packets' busy subloop
// try to spend your time here

Adafruit_MQTT_Subscribe *subscription;
while ((subscription = mqtt.readSubscription(5000)))
{
  if (subscription == &relay)
  {
    Serial.print(F("Got: "));
    Serial.println((char *)relay.lastread);
    if(strcmp((char *)relay.lastread, "ON") == 0)
    {
      digitalWrite(rel,HIGH);
      Serial.println("Relay Turned ON");
    }
    if(strcmp((char *)relay.lastread, "OFF") == 0)
    {
      digitalWrite(rel,LOW);
      Serial.println("Relay Turned OFF");
    }

  }
}

// Now we can publish stuff!
float h = dht.readHumidity();
```

Will give me the value of the feed. I have written some code here that if string compare that will last it is on. Then I will turn on the relay and with the message I'll see that if the extension computer string comparison of the relay not lost luster the value it's off. Then return of the end will simply print on the terminal literally has been done. If you have multiple ones, simply repeat this if loop next time your subscription would be sitting in reality, things like that. So this is my subscription park and ziggurat here. And then here it is. I'm reading the humidity, I'm reading the temperature. And then simply, if not temperature not published, it wins what I'm bussing or I'm calling the function temperature not published. This is the food name and this is the function and passing behind you at speed here. If it does a nonzero value, then it simply means it has been page. So it's not temperature of less than ten, in other words. It is okay. Similarly, my second value humanity seem to if altruism has been exuded here.

If you have some of the values which you have of losing, you have to defeat these two evils. Things. Here. I publish the impression he never missed humidity. And then I'm printing some asterisks, and I'm taking a delay of 5 seconds. And after the IOC ends, we have 2 seconds of the middle console. One. Thank you for time. Let's make it three. And lastly, this is the amputee connect function. Don't make any changes to it. It will simply check if it is connected. If it is connected, it will simply return. If it is not connected, it will try to connect to the. And the code is pretty strict, simple and straightforward. All I am going to do now is I'm going to upload this into the board. I will see the output. So let's do that in our next project when we have the camera ready to check.

# ADAFRUIT PROJECT - PART 3

Now my quote uploading is in process. I have just done the camera turning on and you can see let me just set it once. Okay. So connecting to robotics lab. This is my heart. A bit connected. I got an IP address. Then it is not yet connected. So it is a train duty and also connected. Let's just go through here. This will see some values over here coming. So humidity, it's 50. 60 and temperature is 29. 90. And the same values we should be able to observe over here. However, we are not. So temperature is correct. You would. It is not correct. Let's see. What is the problem with humidity? I'll go to Dashboard. Let's just do the shoot again.

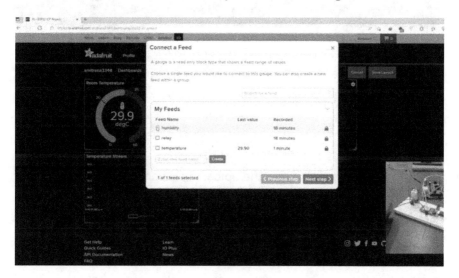

So what is the problem with this roadblock? It's connected to humidity, food. Next step. 0 to 100. All looks good here. So foods you read Dee dee, dee dee. Keep in mind if everything is good with this filename so we can see temperature but we can not see humidity. Okay. I can understand the reason. The reason is very simple. We have published them back.

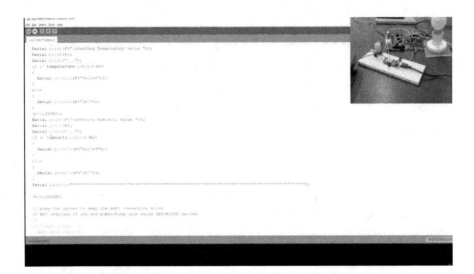

Me? You shouldn't be doing that. So let me just put a delay here of 3 seconds. So it is basically throttling the the free account is throttling because I'm trying to send two valuesback to back. So if I did deliver beer, I should reduce this. But just let's keep it as it doesn't matter. So we have sent temperature and then we are waiting and then we will send humidity. Now let's wait for the record to be uploaded. So connecting uploading is in progress. Once the uploading is done, the serial terminal will become active. We get to see some status connecting to the working slab connected connecting to MQ duty failed retrying and due to connection in both the connected. Now it will send temperature first and then it will appear 29. 90%. Then humidity 50. 00 is also okay. Now, let's refresh this one over here. Now, as you can see, we have both the pilots. You have temperature here and we have the humidity over here as well. Now, let us also try this switch.

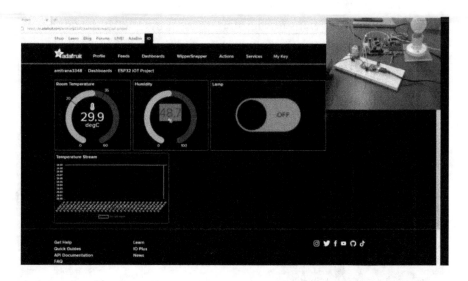

So the switch is basically supposed to push back some values. So I'll just keep this one over here. Let's skip all three windows here. So there is switch. It is still terminal. And here is the. All. So I'll just turn this lamp to on position. You can see. Got on. Really turn on. Can you see how instantaneous that was? It was a few of the billions we have in our program. See that. So fast. Now, this is just one thing. Okay. If you see, I don't have or I have not utilized this on board illegally over here, and I can do that as well. If you have to do a list of changes, what you will do, it's in. So let's let me take LSD and let's call it a lady and the school building. Okay. I'll just use a little bit in the name itself. So SEPTA. Been more. And underscored belief in Goma output. And let's do digital right entity. And those were built in Goma. Look, I'm very doubtful whether this is too high or too low, but let's do it this way. So now that we have it in there, we will also have another feed. Emily let's call it anything like that. Okay. Changes in the code you have subscribe to relay here. So you will subscribe to entity here. And here we will just repeat this. So I told you, the reason I'm showing this to you is because if you want to make changes and if you get stuck somewhere, then this should help. So subscription and really. And they did not lasted. And they did not last through here in this building. Then it lasted, and then here and under school, built in. So we have everything written as a change to the code for LSD and stuff related on it should be turned on and turned off and everything is done over here. I will also reduce this genius furthermore to let's say, 1500. So that will see further, faster court execution. And while this court has been applauded, what we will have to do is, you know, we will have to go here. And we will have to create a new block and connect to a field on a new field called Ellie.

Let's take a toggle switch and let's create a new feed called entity. We can create the feed directly over here. So let's call it relative unknown. Then the button has been created, inserted below. Let's stick it over here. Let's review some sites so that they look a bit business. And save the lunch. Now let's check whether we have the code uploaded. Yes, it is uploaded. And immaturity is also connected. And potential value is coming your way. Then it's come. Let's start again. Lam turning on your city. It's. And is the happening on? Okay. We'll have to close the lamb to check then, but I guess you have seen it. So if you sugarcoat the reality, it's no fun. Any return off.

And the return on. Lantern on, lantern off. So that it's, my friends, a complete project that you can build with the research you do and some simple components. Now again, there are a number of different things that you can do in IO, but we'll see that in our next.

# ADAFRUIT PROJECT - PART 4

Hi. Now that we have seen a complete project over here with idea, let's go a bit more in deep two. Okay. So you have seen that you can have a line chart, but a gauge and no values like that.

You can have multiple different. Balance multiple different charts over here. So you can also have a stream of data coming here, line chart coming here and things like that. Now, if I go, let's say to room temperature, particularly this one here, then I will be able to see the inset chart off temperature values right over here, if you can see. So usually in an industrial or any real time, I will not find the data being sent so fast. Okay. We usually send once some minutes or not even months of my expectations for compliance so far have been sending data once, 5 minutes, 10 minutes or 15 minutes. That's usually fine. Now. Again, if you don't want to purchase it, I'll and if you have to share this to your client or with your customer, you can do that. How? Let's, for example, this is something you have created and you want to give your client access to this. You want him or her to see this, but you don't want to give them any access to this controlling mechanism. But they should be able to look at the look and feel of this. What you can do in that case is just go to this. That's what it is, controls. You will see that it's not more load just to make your look and feel the way you want. But the important point here is

Dashboard. So currently it is locked. If you unlock it, it will make all your friends public and you can simply share this link to a client and they can access it. Let's see a demo. So what I'll do is I'll just open any other browser. Locally, it's still better. So we have not logged in here, and I'll just press this link over here. And we will see. We can still see the dashboard. To see streaming data on designs you will need to create telecoms. I don't want to create an account, but I can see something over here that gives me an access to it. Okay. I can also click on let's see, temperature stream and I can see all the values over here. If you notice, you will not see or even not get any more details like downloading or anything.

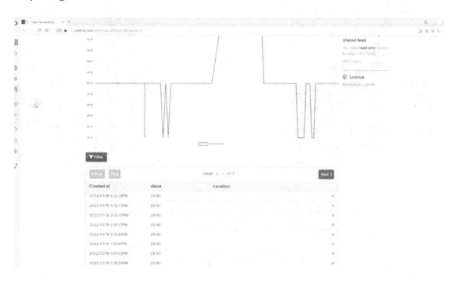

However, this is a good start. You can give this to anyone. Just stresses. It's definitely control. Actions will not be available. Moreover, if you go into your food, any particular food, just like things, you will get a facility to download your data. You can download it as JSON or add CAC. Most of the times your client will do this on their card if they want to do something about it. If they want to experiment, something about it. And as I said, the basic analytics is present over here as well. So if I go back to my dashboard, this is my change that leaves you the way you want. Now, let me go to the actions part. So let's review on what actions are available. There is no action currently and yet in three account. So we have limited actions available. There are two types of actions. One is the reactive action and another one is a scheduled action, serial action. It's something which you may like to do once a day or twice a day or something like that. Reactive action. It's something of an analytical action that. Let's see if. My favorite temperature. Is greater than. Let's see. 31, then. Action. So what's your message to. Somewhere or some food or send a message that you can create a web hook for any other application.

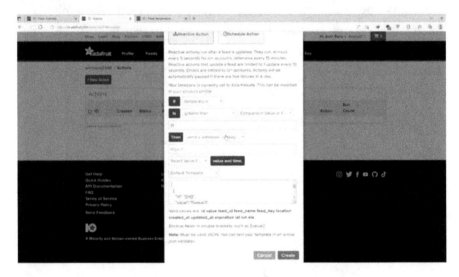

But in your broken. You can also see the email action. So just want to hear. Emily Currently this is a basic enough for my account, but a broken. If you create then you can also send emails to yourself from here. So pro account is not that expensive. Even with enough radio, it gets $10 per month and Alabama is a much, much affordable. What you can see back if you consider a customer, primarily an industrial customer for that matter. Okay. So this is about it. I hope you will experiment a lot with it. And I'm going to keep the synths running for my next experiment. So I want to use Alexa to simply control my lap.

# ALEXA BASED LAMP CONTROL

Hi. In this experiment, what we are going to do is we are going to control this lamp based upon a command given to the speaker. I have on purpose muted my somewhat now because if I don't, I'm going to use Alex similar many times in this project and maybe it will cause issues. So this is an echo dot simplest small Amazon Alexa compatible speaker and what I'm going to do is I'm going to control this lamp using the commands given to Echo. Now how do we do that? Let's see.

## Things you'll need

- Alexa echo or alexa app
- IFTTT account
- Adafruit IO Account and the Same last Arduino Code

So for this experiment, what you're going to need is either you need to have an Amazon Alexa Echo or an Alexa app in your smartphone. Then you are going to have this particular account on the service called I. Typically, I have quality is very interesting and we can do many things with it will see that one by one in this project. And then lastly, you're going to have the same old enough account and the same code, exactly the same code which we did in our last. Where do you just let us open it. So I ordered it four dot com. The thing is that it's still there. The same dashboard is working. I'm not going to do any changes to the program still may be able to use. And so how the flow is very interesting. Let's see how it will work. It will work in this way. So first thing is we will create a word for Alexa. This will be sent to the server or a service called availability after quality will then forward this command to the data from the broker.

## Flow

- Alexa sends command to IFTTT Server
- IFTTT Will send command to adafruit broker
- Adafruit Broker will update the value of relay feed
- Esp32 is subscribed to relay feed to it receives it
- ESP32 turns on/off relay

Informed worker will then updated the value of my related. Since SD 32 has subscribe to the live feed. It will receive that value and the lamp will turn on, so a signal will initiate from here. Go first to Amazon server from Amazon server to availability from. I extrapolated enough the data from a different IO to back to my ask you to and to the lab and we'll see how it works. That is the reason we don't have which is the code isn't so interesting. I don't have to change the world at all. It's a completely different project, completely different code. You're going to use it for control. Let's see how we do that. Okay. So yeah, I'm a little bit excited if you sense in my voice. Unusual, but it is that interesting. So. Let's open after 20 dotcom. And what do you need to do when you go to CNN Politics. com? It's you simply have to create a free account with you. So a creation is very simple. Just put the log in or continue with Apple, Google or Facebook, things like that. I have created my log in here, so simply log in. Do I have to? Now this camera will create some problems. Just a minute. Let me see if I can turn the camera off for some time. I think I can. Okay, great. Now when you go to I have to build the service is very simple and Norway we need to unify. You see 90 blocks created for tutorials on Africa, but I don't know how to do that. I want to directly jump and do some experiment with it because it is that simple. Okay, so let's do something. What you don't have to do is you create an applet. I don't know why the call it is applied and certified, but because it is not a complete app. There's just an app. It's. I'm not going for a pro account.

 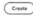

## Start connecting your world.

Get more

I will just use a free account. So simply go to create a button and start creating an applet. The v i property box is very simple. If this here it can check some particular thing happening then that. So I f the data. If this then that that's life. So when you click on. Create. You will get to the screen. So if this then that next add something if this. And you know what we want to add here, right? We want to add Amazon Alexa. So you have to have an Amazon account to do that.

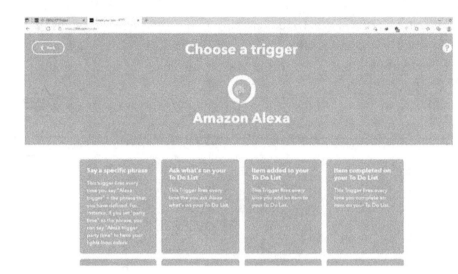

What you will do is you will choose A to Amazon Alexa. Then a number of different triggers created over here. I don't want any of them. So what I want is see a specific fruits. Just use this one. Now it will ask you to connect this particular service to your Amazon account so people connect. And here you will have to log into your Amazon account. It will automatically search for your Alexa device and you'll be connected. This two step verification is theirs. So let me just put the OTP Set seven two for W6 now. Alexa, it's connected over here. Click. Allow to sign in to obtain. So set up specific threats which are suck on Amazon. This is my Alex. I've got what threats. Let's do what. Lamp on. Okay. That's it. That's what I want. Land on. So my first step is done. If I send them on, on my equal or Alexa, then something should happen. What should happen? Let's look at here now as you can judge, what I want to do is I want to chose this service called in with you. And I want to send some data to. So I'll choose a different aisle I'm going to have and have to connect to enough mobile so user enough account credentials and simply authorize this connection. Now Richard after the count amygdala which Friedman temperature not we're not going to center temperature and we're not to send this lamp on to really. And what data you want to send it here on. So that will create an action. Continue.

If You say "Alexa trigger lamp on", then Send data to relay feed

Receive notifications when this Applet runs

Finishing...

So if you see an example, trigger alarm on. Then send it out to the elephant variable. Let's finish this one. Now I have connected to my board Amazon in a different account over here. So I have created one to turn on the lamp. I'll have to create another applet. So if this. The services again. Amazon, Alexa. Say a specific phrase. This is the tree that I want to use. Same account. What phrase I want to use now. So lamp on we have given. Let's choose lamp off here. So create a trigger then that let's choose a of service here. Cyndi Lauper. Dion Yes. Not the temperature of the field, but the same the cliff edge. And here. Now I want to save the data off. And clearly the action. So we have two actions created. One is an acceptable plan, and another one is to get them off. Now, let me open my recorder. So let's turn on the camera so that you have access to Alexa as well as the lamp. Now will do one more thing over here. This. Let's keep our dashboard here in The View. Okay.

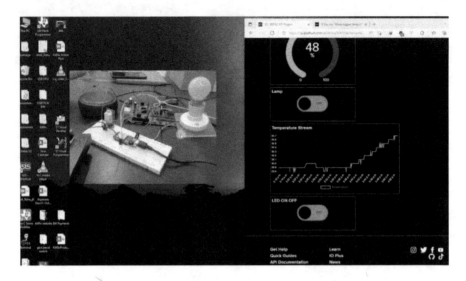

So that we can see the status of this lamp sooner changing. Now that we have created the app, let's try it. Let's do that. Let's see if it works or if it doesn't. Now let's give it a try. So what we'll do is we'll just write a new data account on our Alexa over here. And let's say the friends. Alexa trigger lamp on. Sending back to it. It will. The lamp, it's on here. And you can see the bulb turning on. Alexa.

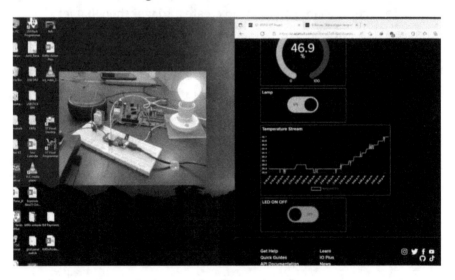

So I'm having trouble destroying the little one. Alexa Trigger lamp off. Sending them to eight. Office not received. I guess that it's some issue. Alexa Trigger lamp off. Sending them to eight. Here. You can see the lamp trigger got off and Atlanta's done. So you can also do something turn off or something like that. So you got to turn off the lamp, off something like that. Anything will do again. Let's give it a try. Alexa, do you ever lamp on? Sending them to eight. Alexa trigger lamp off. Sending that to it. Now we are not monitoring any of it and we can see the lamps being controlled pretty nicely through Alexa. So I'm just making it a mute statement again throughout this project because I'm using Alexa a lot of things. So this is a comfortable device? I don't think so. You need any specific knowledge or anything in order to use this thing? It's very simple. You can create as many appliances you want in your free account. Do you have, I guess, four or five applets available? So you can do this much over here, but you can also create email triggers and also create a lot, many such different things with you. Again, if you are a professional developer or trying to become a professional developer or maker, I think I started my pro trials. I don't want that installment. I think my card account information is on the card. I will be charged. Okay. So it was what I was saying was, if you are a professional who is into creating projects, then having $10 per month for availability and $10 per month on the service like things big enough with IO. Can do wonders for you. You can create and develop as many projects as you want using this particular. So I guess that's about it.

Username

amitrana3348

Password

••••••••••••••••

Change password

Email

amitrana3348@gmail.com

So let's just try it one more time before we shut down for this particular experiment. Alexa trigger lamp on. Sending that to. Alexa Trigger lamp off. Lucy is to be judged at a her. Oh, my goodness. They're going to love this and they're going to play it like forever or something. So that's it for this project, guys. Keep experimenting and keep me posted of any doubts you may have. The setup at scene again for this project. Let me show you if I have forgotten the sulky. It is also saying there is no change at all. That's all you have to create.

www.ingramcontent.com/pod-product-compliance
Lightning Source LLC
LaVergne TN
LVHW051345050326
832903LV00031B/3757